LISTENING SKILLS SCHOOLWIDE

ACTIVITIES AND PROGRAMS

THOMAS G. DEVINE
University of Lowell

ERIC Clearinghouse on Reading and Communication Skills
National Institute of Education

National Council of Teachers of English
1111 Kenyon Road, Urbana, Illinois 61801

Book Design: Tom Kovacs

NCTE Stock Number 29560

Published 1982 by the ERIC Clearinghouse on Reading and Communication Skills and the National Council of Teachers of English, 1111 Kenyon Road, Urbana, Illinois 61801

This publication was prepared with funding from the National Institute of Education, U.S. Department of Education, under contract no. 400–78–0026. Contractors undertaking such projects under government sponsorship are encouraged to express freely their judgment in professional and technical matters. Prior to publication, the manuscript was submitted to the Editorial Board of the National Council of Teachers of English for critical review and determination of professional competence. This publication has met such standards. Points of view or opinions, however, do not necessarily represent the official view or opinions of either the National Council of Teachers of English or the National Institute of Education.

Library of Congress Cataloging in Publication Data

Devine, Thomas G., 1928–
  Listening skills schoolwide.

  Bibliography: p.
  1. Listening—Study and teaching. I. ERIC
Clearinghouse on Reading and Communication Skills.
II. National Council of Teachers of English.
III. Title.
LB1065.D37   1982   428.3   82–14419
ISBN 0–8141–2956–0

CONTENTS

LIST OF FIGURES

FOREWORD

The Educational Resources Information Center (ERIC) is a national information system developed by the U.S. Office of Education and now sponsored by the National Institute of Education (NIE). It provides ready access to descriptions of exemplary programs, research and development efforts, and related information useful in developing more effective educational programs.

Through its network of specialized centers or clearinghouses, each of which is responsible for a particular educational area, ERIC acquires, evaluates, abstracts, and indexes current significant information and lists this information in its reference publications.

ERIC/RCS, the ERIC Clearinghouse on Reading and Communication Skills, disseminates educational information related to research, instruction, and personnel preparation at all levels and in all institutions. The scope of interest of the Clearinghouse includes relevant research reports, literature reviews, curriculum guides and descriptions, conference papers, project or program reviews, and other print materials related to all aspects of reading, English, educational journalism, and speech communication.

The ERIC system has already made available—through the ERIC Document Reproduction System—much informative data. However, if the findings of specific educational research are to be intelligible to teachers and applicable to teaching, considerable bodies of data must be reevaluated, focused, translated, and molded into an essentially different context. Rather than resting at the point of making research reports readily accessible, NIE has directed the separate clearinghouses to work with professional organizations in developing information analysis papers in specific areas within the scope of the clearinghouses.

ERIC is pleased to cooperate with the National Council of Teachers of English in making *Listening Skills Schoolwide: Activities and Programs* available.

Bernard O'Donnell
Director, ERIC/RCS

PREFACE

More and more, teachers and parents are concerned about student listening skills. "Students aren't learning as much as they could," it is said, "because they don't know how to listen purposefully and accurately; they are going to be in trouble later—on their jobs and even in their homes—because they don't listen well." Increasingly, teachers ask, "How can we improve student listening skills? How can we tie in listening instruction with study in the content areas? with reading? with the other language arts? In what ways does listening relate to attention? to IQ? What are the best ways to teach critical listening?"

Fortunately, answers do exist for such questions. Researchers have investigated listening and listening instruction; teachers have created and tried out teaching strategies in their classrooms; psychologists have begun to fit the pieces from research and actual classroom practice into a picture that makes sense. At last, a coherent view of the listening process is emerging. A substantial body of theoretical and research literature and an impressive number of descriptions of actual teaching practices in the area of listening are available to teachers today.

It is the purpose of this book to pull together as much of the theory, the research findings, and the descriptions of successful classroom experiences as possible. Indeed, students do not listen as well as they could, which should concern teachers and parents. However, listening problems are now being defined and addressed, and some possible solutions are available. General background information is presented in the first chapter; specific ideas for teaching activities and programs are developed in chapters two through five.

1 THE IMPORTANCE OF LISTENING INSTRUCTION

Many teachers are concerned about listening, and many parents share their concern. Complaints such as these are regularly heard:

"These boys and girls simply don't listen!"

"They cannot follow basic directions!"

"I may as well talk to the walls!"

Those teachers who have reviewed research findings in the field may agree, yet ask: "But have we *taught* them to listen? Have we shown them how? Have we given them practice?" Teachers who have informally experimented with listening instruction and have become enthusiastic about its potential like to remind complainers that students cannot usually do square roots without some instruction or even drive automobiles well without purposeful (and guided) practice. They note that swimming may be "natural" but that swimmers respond well to coaching and practice.

Listening instruction in most schools has been neglected. The reasons for its neglect are many and varied, but one explanation stands out: listening skills are taken for granted. Listening is such an intrinsic part of schooling that few educational theorists and planners have bothered to examine it within the total context of teaching and learning. It is so basic to the educational enterprise that most learning theorists are not conscious of it. It plays such a supportive role in the daily drama of most classrooms that many teachers overlook it. Listening—the most used and perhaps most important of the language (and learning) arts—has been lost sight of in the business of running schools. Familiarity may or may not breed contempt; it surely leads to fuzzy focus and forgetfulness.

Teachers should be concerned about listening. It is crucial to students in school as well as later in their lives, and researchers are now turning their attention to it. Five important characteristics of listening have been identified, and a discussion of these characteristics will provide teachers with the background for the activities in the following chapters.

Important Characteristics of Listening

One reason listening has not been taught in schools is that it has not been carefully characterized and defined. Listening means too many things to too many people. Fortunately, researchers and specialists in language arts have gathered enough background information so that teachers may begin to develop effective programs.

Listening Is Central to All Learning

In what seems to have been the first formal study in the area, Paul Rankin, in 1927, followed children, adolescents, and adults through the activities of their daily lives to discover which of the language arts predominated. He discovered that people did not really write much: only 9 percent of their total time devoted each day to verbal communication was spent with pen, pencil, or typewriter. (And this figure may have been inflated by the number of students in his sample.) The people in Rankin's study devoted about 16 percent of their time to reading. About 30 percent of communication time was spent speaking, but about 45 percent was spent listening. Since Rankin, other researchers have compared these figures with different populations, in different places, at different times. The results come out about the same: people, generally, listen more than they read, write, or speak. More recently, Miriam Wilt did a similar study in classrooms. She timed all class activities in elementary schools, hour by hour, day by day, and discovered that children spend almost 60 percent of their classroom time listening. Other studies done with secondary school students indicate at least this much time is spent listening in junior and senior high school classrooms. Studies in recent years examining the effects of wide use of radio and television support the belief that ours is a society of listeners. (For specific references, see Devine, 1978.)

These statistics assume added significance when one realizes the peculiar impact of listening. Readers have opportunities to go back and forth on the printed page, to think through new information and ideas at their leisure, and to accept or reject material as they choose. Listeners are bombarded with spoken data, which they have little time to criticize before assimilating. This characteristic of listening makes listeners especially vulnerable. It is possible for skillful but unprincipled speakers to shape personal opinion, affect behaviors, and influence attitudes and values. As many teachers have observed, "The professional persuaders, whether politicians, advertisers, pleaders of causes, or barkers at country fairs, have learned with Hitler, that 'It is in their listening that people are most vulnerable.' Yet while speakers have developed the skills of persuasion, listeners in general have not learned to listen, especially listen critically" (Devine, 1978, p. 299).

Listening Can Be Taught

Hundreds of studies have been done on listening in the past decades, most of which have focused upon its teachability. All have demonstrated that listening skills can be taught. At this point, there seems little doubt about the teachability of basic listening skills. A teacher who sets out, for example, to teach seventh-grade students how to follow spoken directions will probably succeed. Structured lessons, spaced over a period of time and using reasonably interesting examples, will work. Two studies from the 1950s are worth noting here. Sister Mary Hollow set out to teach fifth graders four listening skills: drawing inferences, recalling facts in sequence, remembering facts accurately, and summarizing. She pretested 600 students, gave thirty twenty-minute lessons to half the group, and followed the school's regular language arts program with the other half. When retested, students in her experimental group scored higher on the listening test, and she was able to demonstrate statistically that these elementary children could, indeed, be taught to listen better. Another well-known study in listening was done by Charles Irwin at Michigan State College. He gave listening instruction to students in four sections of freshman composition and, at the end of seven weeks, tested these students against four sections that had not been given listening help. Irwin concluded that "a sufficient number of processes involved in listening can be positively influenced by teaching as to result in improvement in

listening" (Devine, 1978, p. 298). Studies similar to these have been replicated so often that teachers can be fairly sure that they are not wasting student time when they set out to teach listening skills. (For a further discussion of these studies, see Devine, 1978.)

Listening Is Not Simply Attention

A great many theories have been developed by psychologists to explain attention. One widely accepted theory suggests that attention is a limited mental resource. An explanatory metaphor says it is an "energy limitation": attention is powered by a fixed electrical current, allocable to only so many tasks. According to this notion, when the current is spread too far, a fuse is blown. Attention, as many contemporary cognitive psychologists interpret it, is "single-minded"; that is, one cannot focus well on two matters at once, and one cannot perform two demanding tasks simultaneously (Anderson, 1980). Is listening simply attention? Most researchers in this area say no. However, most agree that attention has much to do with successful listening. Clearly, listening involves more than attention but is impossible without attention.

Examples in later chapters clarify this important distinction. Two specific examples are given here. In the first, Mary is tested for recall of data in an experiment in short-term memory conducted in a university psychological laboratory. The experimenter flashes a combination of letters on a screen (such as ADF) and then recites verbally a string of somewhat similar letter combinations (ABD, AFD, FAD, ADC). When Mary hears the original combination, she is supposed to ring a bell. Is her success contingent upon her attention or her listening ability? A reasonable answer must include both. Mary must be paying attention and must be listening. However, the nature of listening in this case may be termed low-level. Mary needs only to recognize the phonemes and recall the order in which they were flashed on the screen. Several perceptual and cognitive tasks are demanded, but they are categorized as low-level in relation to those confronting the listener in the next example.

Bob has taken his first job in a neighborhood service station. His new boss fires this string of phonemes at him the first morning:

> Go around back where I keep the new stuff. Find that case of synthetic motor oil and take out two cans for the display case. Put the rest in the pit where Charlie

is working and then go over to the Mobil station across the street and get that wrench that clown Herb borrowed three weeks ago.

Does this speech demand attention? Does it challenge Bob's listening skills? Both answers must be affirmative. Bob must pay attention. And because attention is, as the psychologists say, "single-minded," Bob cannot listen to the words of his favorite song being played on the station stereo or wave to his friend driving down the main street or speculate on his chances of persuading his favorite girl to go dancing, if he is paying attention to his boss. But here, so different from the laboratory situation discussed earlier, other aspects of listening play roles. An experienced listening teacher analyzing the tasks facing Bob will find that he must use several well-defined listening skills:

Listening to note details
Listening to follow sequence
Listening to identify main points
Listening to note inferences
Listening to recognize speaker bias

Listening, when analyzed this way, becomes a composite of processes extending beyond paying attention. Bob must convert spoken sounds to "meaning in the mind" (Lundsteen, 1979, p. 1); he must do some rather high-level *thinking* as he follows the spoken directions of the service station manager.

Listening Is Related to Thinking

The relationship between listening and thinking is still being studied by researchers, but at this point it seems clear that many of the operations involved in listening—especially higher-level kinds of listening—are mental operations. Listening at its most basic level is simply a matter of processing the incoming meaningful sounds into syntactical and larger units so that the listener may make sense of the sounds. Listening at its basic level is like decoding in reading. However, thinking and the mental operations associated with it are involved in both decoding and listening. An examination of the listening skills Bob needed in his first day of work at the service station helps to explain the relationship between listening at its higher levels and thinking. "Listening to note details" is more akin to attention. "Listening to identify main points" and "Listening to note inferences" sound

more like topics from a college freshman logic book.

Frequently, a teacher who says, "You are not listening to me," really means, "You are not thinking along with me." High school and college students who listen well to lectures may be said to be thinking along the same lines as the lecturer. Several years ago, James Moffett noted, "If a reader can translate print into speech—read it aloud as sentences with normal intonation patterns—and still fail to grasp the idea or relate facts or infer or draw conclusions, then he has no *reading* problem; he has a *thinking* problem, traceable to many possible sources, none of them concerning printed words" (Moffett, 1968, p. 16). Miriam Wilt, a researcher in listening, extends this argument to cover listening and not comprehending and concludes that the listener has a thinking problem (see Devine, 1978). In chapter four on critical listening, these matters are explored in greater depth. It is enough to note here that listening is much more than simply paying attention; listening involves facets of reasoning and thinking of a very high order.

Listening Is Not the Same as Intelligence

Earlier researchers wondered if listening might be directly related to intelligence. Observations in the classroom revealed that "smart kids" seemed to pick up more of the teacher's spoken messages than their counterparts at the other end of the bell-shaped curve. Some suggested that the ability to listen well was an aspect of IQ. Correlational studies found coefficients ranging from .22 to .78 between scores on standardized listening tests and IQ tests. Early critics of these studies noted, however, that such high coefficients were to be expected because both listening and intelligence tests involve language comprehension and the interpretation of verbal symbols. Overlapping, they said, should be expected. Enough variance existed in scores of both kinds of tests *not* accounted for by elements common to both to conclude that listening did depend upon something besides intelligence. Since these studies, so much criticism has been focused upon the standardized intelligence tests that the argument now seems out-of-date. At present, no one knows beyond the shadow of a reasonable doubt exactly what intelligence is. It may be said that intelligence is a combination of *thinking skills*. (And many authorities say that such cognitive skills are teachable.) Listening teachers may set out with good professional conscience to teach students to think more effectively through their listening lessons. (For more on this topic, see Devine, 1981.)

The Need for a Scope and Sequence of Skills

Effective programs are generally built upon a carefully sequenced structure of learnings. A successful listening program also needs such underpinnings. Before examining lessons and strategies, it is necessary to look at a suggested scope and sequence and the rationale underlying it and to review some of the recent discussion of skills-based program development.

The Controversy over Order of Comprehension

At the present time, discussion continues among reading specialists about whether reading is best viewed as a top-to-bottom or bottom-to-top activity. Those who take the first view say readers confront the total text, pick out possible clues within it, and go directly to the author's message. Traditional reading skills, to these authorities, are constructs of the reading teacher that have little or no importance to the child learning to read. *Skills* to reading specialists holding this view is an ill-chosen, almost unnecessary term. "We don't teach boys and girls reading skills," they say; "we teach them to read!" The more traditional bottom-to-top reading specialists still recommend that young children learning to read be taught discrete reading skills in some defensible order—"Children first need to follow a sequence before they can begin to select key ideas; then they go from main ideas to details, and from these basic comprehension skills to higher-level reading skills."

This debate among reading specialists has clear implications for teachers of listening. Do listeners take in total communications and work back in their minds to the details, or do they work from discrete listening skills to the larger context? The two points of view and the various attempts to reconcile them have occupied considerable space in research journals and will continue to engage the attention of researchers in the field. However, the assumption underlying any program for developing listening ability is that *for teaching purposes* listening is best viewed as a composite of separate teachable skills. Listeners may derive meaning from

larger structures of spoken discourse, but teachers of listening can best *teach* the total process by focusing upon one or two skills at a time.

Listening teachers who accept this basic assumption are faced with two difficult questions: What are the specific skills in listening? What is the best order for sequencing them? The first question may be answered based on five decades of research in listening: most teachers and researchers have agreed that specific listening skills are at least somewhat comparable to basic reading skills. A teacher who wants to set up a program in listening may start by examining the reading skills listed in one of the popular basal reading series. Each of the basic reading skills may be translated into a basic listening skill. For example, three basic reading skills selected from a seventh-grade teacher's manual accompanying one basal reader may easily be rephrased into related listening skills:

> Recognizing an author's main ideas
> Following an author's sequence of ideas
> Noting an author's bias

become

> Recognizing a speaker's main ideas
> Following a speaker's sequence of ideas
> Noting a speaker's bias

It should be noted that no one knows if these are indeed the basic listening—or reading—skills. As more and more research is done in both fields, present lists will be refined; some items will be added and some deleted. It may be said, with a modicum of confidence, that a comparison of accepted reading skills can lead to a working list of comparable listening skills so that teachers who want to start teaching listening in their classes may say, with some assurance, "Let's start *here!*" Debates about top-to-bottom and bottom-to-top approaches to reading instruction are important. However, the individual teacher who wants to design a program to improve listening skills cannot wait for the research and theory to be settled to the satisfaction of all. The eager teacher of listening may as well start at the teachable beginning: "Here are some basic listening skills that no one can quibble about; let's teach them."

One problem remains. What is the best order? Separate lessons, exercises, games, and activities scattered throughout the school year represent a kind of shotgun attack on the listening problem. Underlying instruction—from elementary grades through the last year of high school—should follow some coherent framework, a taxonomy or a scope and sequence of well-defined and widely accepted skills arranged from "easiest" to "most difficult." Unfortunately, such a scope and sequence does not yet exist. In her comprehensive study of listening instruction, Sara Lundsteen (1979) examined approaches to the development of progressions on listening skills and looked at tentative hierarchies of both general and critical listening skills. She decided that until much more is known about the cognitive development of children and young adults, a truly definitive listing of skills was impossible.

Basic Listening Skills: A Suggested
Scope and Sequence

The top-to-bottom/bottom-to-top controversy is real and important; its implications for reading and listening instruction are great. However, teachers designing listening programs do need some master plan; otherwise instruction may become random and repetitive. Such a plan (adopted from Devine, 1981) is presented here as a framework for both lesson and program development in listening. It suggests a scope and sequence of basic listening skills.

1. Determining one's own purpose for listening
2. Guessing the speaker's purpose for speaking
3. Following the sequence of ideas
4. Noting details accurately
5. Following spoken directions
6. Guessing the speaker's plan of organization
7. Noting transitional or signal words and phrases
8. Recognizing a speaker's main points or ideas
9. Noting the speaker's supporting details and examples
10. Using a study guide or outline when provided
11. Keeping track of main points by notetaking or mental recapitulation as the talk proceeds
12. Distinguishing between new and old material
13. Distinguishing between relevant and irrelevant material
14. Noting possible speaker bias
15. Noting emotional appeals
16. Distinguishing between fact and opinion
17. Predicting possible test questions in a lecture
18. Recognizing speaker inferences
19. Predicting outcomes of a talk
20. Drawing conclusions from the talk
21. Asking one's own personal questions (mentally or on paper) as the talk proceeds
22. Summarizing the speaker's main points (mentally or on paper) after the talk
23. Relating the speaker's ideas and information to one's own life and interests

An individual teacher may use such a list, however tentative, to plot out lessons. Key skills appropriate for a given grade level may be selected as the basis for a one-year program for one class. Thus, rather than just teaching listening, the teacher can focus on five or ten skills for a particular class for the year. "If nothing else," such a teacher can say, "my students are going to be good at Following a sequence of ideas, Following spoken directions, Noting details accurately, and Recognizing a speaker's main points." A teacher at a higher grade level may say, "My students seem to be pretty good at that sort of listening, but they need help with critical listening; I am going to focus on Noting emotional appeals, Noting speaker bias, Distinguishing fact from opinion statements, and Drawing conclusions from a talk." Groups of teachers may use such a list to plan an entire curriculum in listening. They may choose items that seem appropriate for specific grade levels in their school or system and together plan a series of lessons aimed at each of the skills. Overlapping, redundancy, repetition, and overteaching may not be eliminated—indeed, they perhaps should not be eliminated—but an orderly framework exists for schoolwide instruction. As individuals and groups of teachers work with this suggested scope and sequence, they will surely make changes. They will refine, delete, and add, but they will make their changes within a framework of order.

A Teacher's Self-Assessment Checklist

Teachers initiating listening programs, either schoolwide or in their own classrooms, find self-assessment a productive first step. They ask: "What am I already doing that's valuable? What parts of my present program need to be kept? expanded upon? eliminated? What features of an effective program must I introduce?" The following checklist, developed by a group of secondary school teachers, will aid teachers in assessing their listening programs. Respond to each question with *Hardly ever, Sometimes, Frequently,* or *Most always.*

1. I include listening instruction in my courses.

2. I read professional literature about listening instruction.

3. I attend workshops, conferences, or courses in which listening is discussed.

4. I structure my classroom talk so that student listeners may derive maximum gain.

5. I try to make students aware of listening skills.

6. I compliment good listening.

7. I provide for students a model of a good listener.

8. I refer to listening skills in class discussions of other topics.

9. I teach lecture notetaking skills.

10. I teach my students to
   a. Determine their own purpose for listening.
   b. Guess the speaker's purpose for speaking.
   c. Follow a sequence of ideas.
   d. Note details accurately.
   e. Follow spoken directions.
   f. Guess a speaker's plan of organization.
   g. Note transitional words and phrases.
   h. Recognize a speaker's main points.
   i. Note a speaker's supporting details and examples.
   j. Use a listening study guide.
   k. Keep track of main points by notetaking or mental recapitulation.
   l. Distinguish between old and new material.
   m. Distinguish between relevant and irrelevant material.
   n. Note possible speaker bias.
   o. Note emotional appeals.
   p. Distinguish between fact and opinion.
   q. Recognize a speaker's inferences.
   r. Predict outcomes of a talk.
   s. Draw conclusions from a talk.
   t. Ask personal questions as the talk proceeds.
   u. Make personal associations.
   v. Summarize a speaker's main ideas.
   w. Evaluate the speaker's competence to talk about the subject.
   x. Note use of propaganda.
   y. Predict possible test questions in lectures.
   z. Care about listening skills.

2 TEACHING ACCURATE LISTENING

The line separating listening from attention is a fuzzy one. So-called good listeners sometimes fail to pay attention to speakers, while poor listeners sometimes pay attention yet miss the message. One traditional area of concern for listening teachers, which brings listening and attention together for the purpose of instruction, has been called *accurate listening*. Teachers who develop lessons to promote accurate listening are concerned with such questions as: What classroom activities will encourage students to pay attention? What strategies will force students to heed the details of a talk? How may such activities be related to out-of-school listening? This chapter suggests answers to these important questions.

Some General Suggestions

Ideas for teaching tend to group themselves by grade levels. Some ideas work well with younger children; some appeal to boys and girls in middle school; others are clearly more effective with high school students. However, some general guidelines underlie the development of all classroom activities.

Build lessons in accurate listening into the daily and weekly schedule. Isolated, one-shot activities may be better than none at all, but experienced listening teachers note that lessons need to be regularized. It is better to have one fifteen-minute lesson each week (or one five-minute lesson each day) than to have longer lessons spaced irregularly throughout the school year. Students begin to realize that they can indeed improve their accuracy, that they can become more and more proficient as time passes, that they can learn "not to miss a thing."

Provide for a variety of activities. A teacher who overdoes a specific kind of activity finds that lessons become nonproductive after a few repetitions. Lessons may be simple spoken messages followed by informal testing. Such exercises work. However, the same type of exercise repeated day after day actually leads to *inaccurate* listening. Teachers who succeed in developing accuracy note that they make use of tape-recorded conversations, dramas, demonstrations, radio, television, music, formal lectures (even in the earlier grades), explanations, debates, films, and videotapes. The focus always remains on accuracy in listening, but the situations and tasks differ.

Emphasize good listening behavior. Some students—in all grade levels—have never been introduced to good listening manners. Some have been told, "Be quiet" or "Do not talk when others are talking," but they have not been given systematic guidance in the etiquette of listening. All need to be reminded of the value of a quiet, receptive audience; all need to be shown the futility of listening in a noisy, distracting context. Some teachers take time early in the school year to discuss the importance of old-fashioned politeness, to encourage students to set up standards of listening behavior, and to post student-made codes on the bulletin boards. One eighth-grade class drew up the following set of standards for listening behavior:

A good listener:
  Looks at the speaker.
  Never talks when a speaker is talking.
  Tries not to distract the speaker.
  Shows attention by body English (smiles, frowns, reacts).
  Thinks about what is being said.

Older students seldom make board charts, but they too need to discuss audience behavior and the importance of listener response. Some high school teachers approach the topic through body English: "How do facial expressions assist speakers? What kinds of posture encourage speakers? discourage them? Why is it important to show speakers that you are listening to them?"

Provide a good model. Many successful listening teachers note that part of their success is due to the model they provide. As their students recite formally in class (and chat informally outside of class), these teachers respond politely and attentively, indicating through their facial expressions and body movements that they are indeed listening. They look directly at speakers; they are later able to quote what speakers have said; they put aside record keeping and other paper tasks while their students speak. Such teacher-models show that they value good listening by regularly praising students who catch details of talks and lectures and by commenting positively on the classroom behaviors of good listeners. They signify by their own behaviors and comments that they really believe listening is important and that accurate listening takes effort on the part of listeners.

Make lessons a part of ongoing instruction. Separate listening lessons are necessary. Short units and extended lessons are crucial to the development of listening skills; short daily practice sessions keep skills alive and growing. However, listening instruction cannot be detached from other aspects of the curriculum—it needs to permeate all studies. Listening teachers should note what happens to spelling and writing in some schools: they are taught regularly but separately, and students begin to think that while spelling and writing may be important in English class, they "don't count" in other content areas. Listening does count—in history and science classes and after the dismissal bell. Listening teachers may relate instruction to other facets of schooling and to life by having students:

Practice notetaking skills in their history and science classes

Discuss problems they encounter listening to televised newscasts and other out-of-school listening situations

Carry into content-area classes the listening guides developed in their listening lessons

Report back their observations and examples from other classes and from home

Practice their listening skills on school announcements, radio news and weather forecasts, proclamations, and messages from the principal's office

Teaching Ideas for Middle School and Junior High

Many suggestions for teaching accurate listening may be found in language arts and reading books, in teachers' manuals, and in articles in professional journals. Here are some ideas from earlier grades that may be adopted by middle school and junior

high teachers and some ideas developed specifically for students in those grades.

Sixth-, seventh-, and eighth-graders are not yet too sophisticated to enjoy and profit from strategies regularly used by elementary-grade teachers. Some successful activities that may be adopted for older students focus squarely on accuracy.

The old game of Simon Says is useful because it involves careful listening to directions. A leader gives a command ("Simon says, 'Touch your toes'"), and the group does as it is told. If the leader omits the phrase *Simon says*, students should not obey. Those who follow the command must drop out of the game.

Airplanes Fly is a variation in which students raise their arms and flap them only when the leader mentions something that flies, such as a rocket or hawk. Students have to sit down when nonflying objects are mentioned.

In a more difficult variant, the teacher gives a string of commands, such as: "Arthur, take this chalk to my desk; Susan, take it from the desk and walk with it once around the room; Debbie, you take it from Susan and place it on Tom's desk..."

Another game has the teacher tell a story that includes nonsense information: "The old man walked slowly up the cornstalk and stopped to sit for a minute..." Students are challenged to listen carefully for words that do not make sense.

Middle school and junior high teachers can also rework some of the listening activities in basal reading manuals. Such rhyming games and auditory discrimination exercises are still useful for many upper-grade boys and girls.

The teacher (or child) says: "I rhyme with *rain*. I go on a track. What is my name?" or "I rhyme with *log*. I have a tail. What is my name?"

The teacher starts with a word and students volunteer rhyming words: *bat*, then *cat*, then *mat*, etc.

The teacher tape-records sounds for students to identify: an alarm clock, water from a faucet, a bell, footsteps, a dog's bark, a car horn, etc.

Such simple exercises may be supplemented for some middle school classes with tests on short tales. Students listen for the pleasure of the story. Then the teacher asks four or five simple questions about details to see how accurately students have listened. Once students realize that they may be asked to recall specific information, they tend to listen for details.

Games play a major role in teaching listening to older students as well. Teachers successful at preparing exercises note that the competitive element underlies many of their best listening activities. Directions are given for a few ideas that work.

To encourage accurate listening, read a short, carefully selected magazine article and then ask ten questions about it. Reread the same article (or have a student read it aloud) so that students may correct their own answers. Such "second-chance" listening is useful with passages from textbooks. Students hear the passage once, jot down answers, and then hear it again to double-check their responses. The second-chance aspect of the activity seems to encourage accurate listening during both readings.

In a variation of this second-chance activity, have the students make up questions after they hear a story or textbook passage. Write these questions on the chalkboard and let students listen a second time with the questions before them. The exercise insures involvement, purpose, and accuracy.

To maximize classroom listening, tell students that there will be at least one piece of inaccurate information given during the lecture. Students, who have read the textbook assignment, listen to discover the inaccuracy. They jot down the false information on cards or scrap paper and share it with the class after the formal talk.

To encourage careful listening, try contests. Announce that five points will be awarded after the formal talk or lecture for each piece of information accurately recalled. After the talk, students jot down what they remember, and points are given. The exercise also serves as an effective reviewing strategy.

Divide the class into two relay teams and give each team captain the same written message. Each leader whispers the message to the next team member, who in turn whispers it to the next member. Have the last person write the message down and decide which team has listened most accurately. Good messages might include: "The principal's new car has a flat in the front left tire" or "Today is the fourth anniversary of the day Robert's brother lost his front tooth in a hockey game at Smith Field."

Tape television news. To stay current, the short morning newscasts can be recorded and played back for classes that same day. Students either fill in the blanks on the chalkboard or write *True* or *False* on paper. This is a good way of making students listen to the news and listen for details.

Retell news stories and have students act like reporters and answer the basic questions of when, where, what, why, who, and how. Such activities may be part of junior high units on the newspaper or lessons in writing.

Similar activities may be tied to literature study. After the class has read a selection, give five statements about a character in the book. Students must listen to discover which statement is false, and then they return to the book to verify their hunches.

Try a variant of the "cloze procedure" popular in reading class by taping a passage from the textbook and beeping out key words. Students listen—perhaps two or three times—and decide which words have been deleted. They check their guesses by reading the pas-

sage in the book. This listening exercise is an effective review for a test.

Teaching Ideas for High School Classes

Just as many elementary-grade activities may be adopted for use in middle school and junior high, so may many of the gamelike activities used in these grades be reworked for high school classes. Because of the increasing maturity of high school students, however, instruction might better begin with demonstrations and examples of the importance of careful, accurate listening. One teacher, for example, begins the school year with a discussion of instances in which accurate listening affected actual events. She collected examples of instances in which a listener's failure to heed one or two facts changed the course of people's lives. Some of her examples had to do with economic crises, battles, diplomatic events, political campaigns, and business operations. One particular example concerned a famous rock group that went to the wrong city to perform a concert because someone had listened carelessly to a telephone message. Students in her classes were able to see how misunderstanding one word in a message could influence events. Her introductory unit ended with a research project that sent students into their neighborhoods to collect similar examples for a class publication entitled "It Pays to Listen."

Accurate listening in the high school may be approached in a number of ways: through consciousness-raising devices, direction-following activities, and variations of the simulated newsroom.

Consciousness-Raising Devices

Most people do not always realize that they do not listen accurately. A first step in any program is to make students aware of their bad habits. One high school teacher does this by feeding classes outrageous information: "The 200 million teenagers in the United States are spending more than 50 percent of the total national income on records and tapes" or "As President Roosevelt's jet landed at O'Hare Field, he realized that he had enough votes for the nomination." By delivering impossible data with a straight face, he tricks some of his students some of the time. He comments, "I want to keep their brains twirling throughout every class; after a while, they realize that listeners are responsible for catching every fact, the obvious and the bizarre."

Other teachers have used versions of the Test for Accurate Listening. This is a simple list of items directing listeners to do something. The items are so designed that each listener must attend to details accurately. Some commonly used items on these tests are:

Write the numbers 9, 8, 4, 5, and 7; then circle the largest.

If you circled 8, make a square in the upper-right corner of your paper; if not, make a cross.

If Ronald Reagan is president, write the shorter of the two words *blue* or *black*. If he isn't, write your last initial.

Write the second letter of your last name in the lower-left corner of the paper with a star beside it.

Write the letters *G, D, S, V,* and *T*. Now circle the one that starts with the same sound as a word that appears in the movie title *Star Wars*.

Such exercises need to be long to be effective. Their purpose is to make students realize how much information floats by them in ordinary spoken language. Students begin to see that truly accurate listening is not easy. One teacher encourages students to contribute to an "item bank" of such commands. Once a week, twenty or thirty items are drawn from the bank and presented rapidly to the group. The teacher reminds the students, "We hear words around us all day and stop really listening to them; spoken language is such a part of our common environment that we cease to pay heed to it."

Another consciousness-raising device is the use of a standardized listening test. Many teachers have administered standardized listening tests, such as the Brown-Carlsen Listening Comprehension Test or the STEP Listening Test. Students are allowed to score their own test sheets and compare their scores to national norms. They are often disturbed to discover that they are not listening at their grade level. Other teachers create their own listening tests, selecting a short article from a magazine and preparing twenty questions designed to measure accurate listening. Students listen as the teacher reads the article aloud or listen to a tape recording. They check their answers against the teacher's key and grade themselves. One teacher administers such a listening test each week; students score themselves by percentages and record their weekly scores in notebook charts. They are usually able to see week-by-week improvements and are probably much more conscious of accurate listening than students who never participate in such an activity.

Direction-Following Activities

High school students also need to realize that other kinds of listening are contingent upon accurate listening. Purposeful listening in the classroom, critical listening in front of the television set, and following spoken directions in the shop or science class are all based, to a large extent, upon attention to specific details. One set of activities for helping students understand the primacy of accurate listening grows from giving and following directions. In the following examples, students are given a series of commands.

"You are asked to help out in the school office, and an emergency arises. The principal says: 'A fire has broken out in the basement. I'm running down there. You call Mr. Barnes in the shop. Call his home if he doesn't answer. The number is 576-8967.'" Students are given sets of directions rapidly and asked to pick out what they believe are the essentials. After some practice, students can make up similar exercises and test one another.

"Imagine that you are driving a police patrol car. You get this message on the car radio: 'Accident at Burns and Fifth. Seems to be a fire. Ambulance on the way. Be ready for burns.'" Students are asked to repeat the key points of the message. Discussion may center upon such questions as: Which point is most important? Which matter is to be taken care of first? What words are most important? What should you do? not do?

"You are working temporarily in a local service station. The manager, leaving on a job, says quickly: 'That pump on the right isn't acting properly. Tell customers not to use it. Move them to the other. If you have a chance, call Bob at home and tell him to beat it here. We need him. The number's 987-2378.'" Discussion, again, may center upon such questions as: What should you do first? What's essential? What data do you have to recall? What could a listener misinterpret here? What might a listener not catch? Students may prepare similar messages to test one another. The teacher's point in such exercises, of course, is to help students realize the value of identifying key words and noting them for recall.

The Simulated Newsroom Approach

Here the teacher suggests that the classroom is a television or radio newsroom. Several students are news reporters scattered throughout the community; others are editors and rewrite staff based in the office. As reporters in the field come across news stories, they telephone the information to the main office to be rewritten and broadcast. Clearly, the news staff in the station must be accurate listeners.

In the first stages of this simulation game, the teacher may prepare the stories for reporters to call in: "This is Mendez calling from City Hall. I just talked to the mayor, and he denies strongly the rumor that he has been involved in an automobile accident. He says the story is being circulated by his political enemies. His only car is a brown Chevette, and it is being serviced by the Mobil station near his home in Ashmount. The car in the rumors is a big Caddie. The mayor says he has never owned a Caddie." Stories at this stage may range from the silly to the pedestrian; the teacher should try to pack each with as many details as possible.

In a second stage, the teacher may explain the classic questions of newswriting: who, what, where, when, why, and how? Such a simple structure provides guidance for both speakers and listeners: "A bad fire broke out in the old garage at Andover and Greene Streets. The firemen think it was ignited by kids playing in the neighborhood, but they aren't sure. No one was hurt, but damage will run, they think, to several thousand dollars. Chief O'Neil says a careful check will be made for possible arson, but at this time he doesn't think it was set purposefully."

A third stage has students creating their own original stories. Reporters prepare stories at home or before class and call them in. If possible, students call over the intercom to add to the classroom drama. In all its variants, the simulated newsroom does provide practice in accurate listening.

Interest and Attention

The inescapable truth about accurate listening is that care and attention to details are contingent upon one's interest in the spoken communication. Susan may not catch a single detail in an early morning newscast, but when the announcer reads a list of rainy-day school cancellations, she is sure to pick out the name of her school. Dave may not hear a thing in the noisy school cafeteria, but when someone mentions the cute new girl's name, he catches it. Clearly, people pay attention to what interests them. They tend to listen more accurately, with or without special instruction in school, to those spoken messages that somehow relate to them personally. Awareness of the relationship between attention and interest leads to three classroom guidelines.

Encourage Students to Relate Spoken Material to Their Own Lives

Teachers in all content areas need to emphasize the value of relating new materials to students' own lives. As students take in new information and ideas through classroom talk, they need to seek out items that tie in with their own personalities, past lives, aspirations, problems, concerns. Psychologists point out that new material is most effectively encoded, stored, and later retrieved from memory when it is packaged in some way that is meaningful to the learner. Students who see relationships between what the teacher talks about and their immediate lives tend to take in and retain the information.

One successful listening teacher keeps a large wall chart in the front of the classroom with these questions:

How does this concern *me*?

How does this relate to what I already know?

What does it remind me of?

What can I associate it with?

What crazy things pop into my mind when I think of it?

How can I use these crazy associations to help me remember?

How does this relate to my past? my future?

How does it relate to my life outside of school?

The teacher refers to the chart for both reading and listening lessons. As students read assignments and listen to lectures and other oral presentations, they are reminded to make associations with aspects of their own lives.

Set Up Listening Situations That Involve Students

Interest grows out of personal involvement. Teachers who develop oral language lessons that maximize personal involvement note that listening does improve. "Easier said than done!" some may say. But there are teachers who try never to make a formal classroom presentation without structuring into it some personalizing activity. Some examples from actual classrooms follow.

One literature teacher has students note on paper all points in her lectures that relate directly to their own lives. After each lecture, she allows time for discussion of such questions as "What does this discussion of characterization mean to you? Have you ever noticed a person revealing personal qualities through speech or actions? Do you ever reveal your own inner qualities by the way you speak and act?"

A history teacher, lecturing on Prohibition, asks his listeners to write on cards a personal lesson that they have learned from the nation's futile attempt to legislate against the wishes of a majority of people. Students share their lessons, and the discussion often turns to censorship and the outlawing of drugs. Such discussions enhance his presentation of the topic, and listeners are always much more attentive.

A science teacher, speaking on water pollution, has students concentrate on what they can do as individuals to prevent pollution. They often decide to write letters to Congress, to inspect local ponds and streams, or to write to area newspapers; they invariably listen more carefully.

Encourage Students to Listen with Pen in Hand

Recognizing that attention is related to interest and interest to personal involvement, many listening teachers link lessons in accurate listening with notetaking. They remind students that human memory is fragile and that the best listeners cannot catch and remember everything. These teachers, even in the middle grades, begin guided practice in notetaking. Listening with pen in hand is an excellent way of maximizing attention and capturing on paper vital points of a talk. Some effective strategies for beginning instruction in notetaking follow.

Provide student listeners with a detailed outline of the classroom talk or lecture. (As students listen, they follow the main and minor points, noting the specific details of the speaker.)

Provide incomplete outlines that students fill in as they listen. (Stop talking periodically to check student responses: "Did you get that date? that name? What are the three items that you filled in under the second heading?")

Have student listeners respond to the talk by developing a time line. ("If we start with this event in 1861, what ought to come next in my presentation? Where do you put the next item of information?")

Have students prepare maps as they listen. (Using a rough board drawing as a guide, note events as the talk proceeds and as students develop their own notebook maps: "As the settlers moved westward, they came to the river. Approximately where did they cross? Indicate this on your map as we go along.")

Listening with pen in hand tends to provide a minimal structure for response while allowing for important physical involvement. It is not the complete solution to the problem of inattentive listening, but it does focus the attention of the student listener on the task at hand.

One of the most effective ways of increasing attention through notetaking is the Guided Listening Lesson. This structure, based on the Guided Reading Lesson recommended by reading specialists, is a step-by-step guide through the teacher's lecture. It usually consists of (1) an explanation of the lecture's purpose, (2) an introduction (given before the presentation) of new vocabulary words and difficult concepts, (3) questions for listeners to have in mind as the talk proceeds, and (4) a printed guide to fill in while listening. In a reading lesson, the guide forces student readers to move sequentially through a textbook assignment, noting important points and focusing attention on details that the teacher considers important. In a listening lesson, the guide helps students note key generalizations and details and, similarly, concentrates listeners' attention on matters that the teacher wants them to understand and remember. A Guided Listening Lesson may pull together many of the listening goals of the lesson and reinforce learning of basic listening skills. It may be particularly useful in teaching students to listen for accurate details. A sample lesson used by an eighth-grade social studies teacher follows.

Paul Revere's Ride

Directions to listeners: You are going to hear a short talk on Paul Revere's famous ride. Before the talk begins, read through this guide. Make sure you know what you are listening for.

1. *How well do you pick out main ideas?* After the talk is over, list the five main ideas it contained.

2. *How well do you understand the main point of a talk?* After the talk is over and you have listed the five main ideas, indicate the main point of the entire talk in one or two sentences.

3. *How well do you listen for details?* While the talk is given, try to fill in as many of these details as you can:
   a. Paul left from _____ .
   b. His destination was _____ .
   c. He was accompanied by _____ .
   d. His starting signal was _____ .
   e. On the way he saw _____ ,
      _____ , and _____ .
   f. The date of his ride was _____ .
   g. A famous poem about the ride was written by _____ .
   h. The time when he left was _____ .
   i. The time when he returned was
      _____ .
   j. The weather was _____ .

4. *How well do you follow sequence?* After the talk is over, list in correct order five events that happened during the ride.
5. *How well do you note signal words?* While you listen, jot down five signal words or expressions that the speaker uses (one example from the beginning of the talk is *first*).

Sample Lesson Plans

As an outgrowth of regular class work in dramatics, one sixth-grade teacher uses variations of the following lesson to emphasize accurate listening.

Objective

To encourage students to listen accurately

Behavioral objective

At the end of the class session, each child will be able to recall six specific details from the situation.

Procedures

1. Tell students that they may volunteer to act out the situation they will soon hear.
2. Emphasize that they will hear it only once.
3. Have them listen with pencils in hand to catch every important detail.
4. Tell them this situation:

   An elegant, upper-class woman was driving down the highway one day when she saw a famous fast-food hamburger stand. She had never in her life eaten at such a place, but on this day she was hungry. She told her chauffeur to stop and wait while she went inside to order. She had never been inside such a place before. She was stunned by all the noise and confusion. She had never seen so many children. Dozens of people were in line. Young people behind the counter wore strange hats. Signs were all over the walls. She had no idea how to order or how to get a table, so she watched the people around her very carefully. The girl in the next line ordered a Big Mac and a strawberry milkshake. The boy in front of her ordered three hamburgers and three milkshakes, all chocolate, plus five orders of french-fried potatoes. A child in another line ordered nine hamburgers and nine soft drinks, plus three orders of cookies. The poor lady was flabbergasted! She tried her best.

5. Have students turn their notes facedown on their desks.
6. Allow three or four volunteers to act out the situation.
7. Encourage class discussion of details that the volunteers forgot or failed to hear.

8. Reread the situation while students double-check to see how many details they recorded or failed to record the first time.
9. Ask: "Why is it important to listen to details? What kinds of people need to be especially good listeners? How can you improve your ability to listen more accurately?"
10. After students have had an opportunity to discuss their answers, try a similar lesson on the same day or the following day.

One eighth-grade teacher regularly uses variations of the following lesson to foster accurate listening and to develop creativity.

Objectives

To develop the skill of listening to details

To give students further practice in creative thinking

Behavioral objectives

Each student will be able to reproduce ten specific details from each description heard.

Each student will write a one-paragraph description of a location never before visited.

Procedures

1. Announce: "New Planet Discovered!" Tell the students that they are to imagine the discovery of a new planet and the landing of the first spaceship from Earth on that planet.
2. Point out that the hitherto-unknown planet may have a tropical climate and much vegetation, no water or plant growth, no life resembling ours, or quite dissimilar life.
3. Allow time for students to discuss briefly the possible appearance of the new planet, and then encourage a quiet moment for "forming mental pictures."
4. Set fifteen minutes aside for a writing workshop where students write out descriptions of the new planet as they imagine it.
5. Suggest that each student writer pretend to be the first person from Earth to step foot onto the new planet.
6. Have students rewrite their descriptions from the point of view of the person who will send back to Earth the first description. (This is the time for the teacher to help with spelling, punctuation, sentence structure, editing, etc. Final drafts may be done at home or in a subsequent writing workshop.)

Listening Accurately for Details

Listen carefully for specific directions and mark the following diagram accurately.

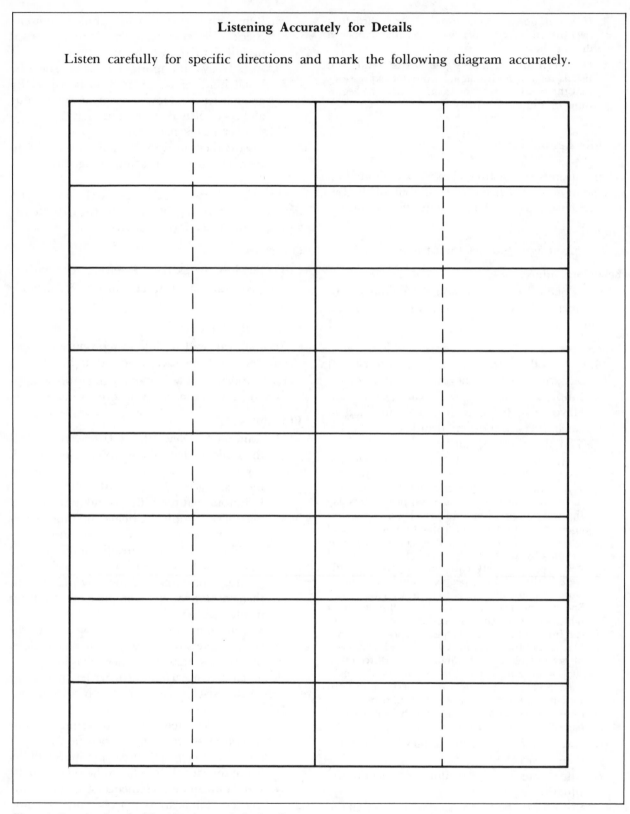

Figure 1. Exercise sheet for Listening Accurately for Details.

7. On another day, six or eight volunteers read their reports aloud.
8. Student listeners (with pen in hand) listen to the volunteers for at least ten details that make the description of the planet unique. (For example, "Instead of being green, all grasses and leaves are bright blue.")
9. If time allows, each volunteer will read his or her description a second (or third) time so that listeners can check their skill in catching details.
10. Each student creates a name for the new planet.
11. The class selects the best description and best name.
12. Outstanding descriptions may be tape-recorded for later use by the teacher as a listening test for the same class later in the year or for other classes.

One high school teacher of English uses a collection of recorded old-time radio programs as the basis for lessons in accurate listening.

Objective

To make listeners attentive to details

Procedures

1. Note that literary scholars often must date newly discovered manuscripts of old poems and novels. ("They can rely on the age of the paper and chemical analysis of the ink and so forth, but they also use details found in the content. For example, if the author mentions railroads or the telegraph, the scholar knows that the piece could not have been written much before the nineteenth century; if the author mentions television, the manuscript was probably written after the late 1930s.")
2. Explain that the class will hear a recording of a popular radio program (such as "The Shadow" or "The Lone Ranger").
3. Challenge individuals in the group to list in their notebooks as much factual data as possible to help date the program.
4. Play the recording.
5. Allow time for students to share their responses.
6. Replay the recording so that students can double-check their findings and locate new examples.

7. Allow additional time for students to compare and discuss the items they have located.
8. Follow up the class activity with this assignment:

Tonight watch and listen to one rerun of an old television series or an old movie. List as many details as possible that might help a future scholar tell approximately when it was filmed.

Exercises

These exercises are designed and presented so that teachers may reproduce them. They are intended to supplement the learning activities in the lessons and to give students increased practice in using important listening skills.

Listening Accurately for Details

This activity leads to exercises in the following chapter for teaching students the important skill of following spoken directions. It may serve as a model for a variety of similar teacher-made exercises.

Students are told to take their copies of the exercise sheet headed Listening Accurately for Details (Figure 1) and to do exactly as directed. The teacher then reads the following directions.

Write your last name in the third square down beside the left margin.
Write your first name in the third square up from the right margin.
Draw a small triangle in the fourth square down to the right of the left dotted line.
Draw a small circle in the second square up from the bottom to the immediate right of the right dotted line.
Make a dot in the third square down from the top to the right of the left dotted line.
Draw a large circle around the top four squares on the left of the page.
Write the day of the week on the topmost line of the entire block of squares.
Write the year in which you were born in the second square up from the bottom to the left of the left dotted line.
Write your initials in the fifth square down from the top, next to the right dotted line.
Put the call numbers of your favorite radio station in the top right-hand corner of the paper. If you have no favorite, write the word *school*.
Place three dots in the fourth square up from the bottom to the right of the right dotted line.

Teachers should complete a master diagram for students to use in checking accuracy of their finished diagrams.

Are You Really Listening?

Check the specific detail that best answers each question.

1. In what year was the ancient Egyptian tomb discovered?
   ____ 1903
   ____ 1922
   ____ 1948
   ____ 1980

2. In what month was it made?
   ____ January
   ____ June
   ____ November
   ____ December

3. How many steps did the archeologists dig down?
   ____ 10
   ____ 12
   ____ 16
   ____ 22

4. What was the passage filled with?
   ____ rubble
   ____ gases
   ____ statues
   ____ jewelry

5. Who was buried in the tomb?
   ____ Lord Carnarvon
   ____ Cairo
   ____ Tut
   ____ Carter

6. In which chamber did they find the pharaoh's remains?
   ____ first
   ____ second
   ____ third
   ____ fourth

7. How old was the pharaoh when he died?
   ____ 10
   ____ 12
   ____ 18
   ____ 22

8. How many coffins was he buried in?
   ____ 1
   ____ 2
   ____ 3
   ____ 4

9. How tall was his burial chamber?
   ____ 9 feet
   ____ 11 feet
   ____ 17 feet
   ____ 10 yards

10. What did they find in the chamber beside the coffin?
    ____ grave robbers
    ____ other pharaohs
    ____ live animals
    ____ furniture

11. What were on the walls?
    ____ rugs
    ____ mirrors
    ____ pictures
    ____ air vents

12. How many packing cases were sent back from the grave?
    ____ 31
    ____ 34
    ____ 41
    ____ 44

13. How many chariots were sent back?
    ____ 1
    ____ 2
    ____ 3
    ____ 4

14. How were the discoveries taken to the Nile River?
    ____ train
    ____ truck
    ____ boat
    ____ mules

15. How many pieces of jewelry were found with the mummy?
    ____ 100
    ____ 123
    ____ 143
    ____ 193

16. Where are these treasures today?
    ____ Cairo
    ____ Rome
    ____ New York
    ____ London

Figure 2. Exercise sheet for Are You Really Listening?

Are You Really Listening?

The second exercise may be used as a pretest, post-test, or consciousness-raising device. The teacher or a student volunteer may read aloud (or tape-record) the following information. Using the multiple-choice quiz, Are You Really Listening? (Figure 2), listeners then test themselves to discover how accurately they listened. The information may be presented a second time to allow listeners an opportunity for second-chance listening.

In November, 1922, two archeologists, Howard Carter and Lord Carnarvon, discovered beneath some workmen's huts a stone step that would lead them to one of the great moments in all scientific investigation. Three weeks of patient digging led them down a flight of sixteen steps to the entrance to a tomb of one of Egypt's ancient pharaohs. There in the Valley of the Kings, they found the lost tomb of Tut, the richest tomb in all Egypt. Beneath the rubble-filled passage, they found a door bearing the ancient royal seal. With trembling hands, Carter made a small hole in the upper left-hand corner. He lit candles to see if there were any poisonous gases and then, slowly, enlarged the hole. There, after centuries, was the magnificence of the long-lost pharaoh's tomb: golden chairs, a diamond-encrusted throne, gold vases, two great statues, and hundreds of priceless jewels. However, nowhere could he or his friends see a sarcophagus or mummy. Could this be the real tomb? they wondered.

In the next days they searched carefully throughout the chamber. Eventually, they located in a rear corner what appeared to be *another* door. They eased this open and found themselves in another chamber, seventeen feet long, eleven feet wide, and nine feet high. Here, between two enormous statues of solid gold, they found Tut, the eighteen-year-old "boy king." The mummy was in a gold coffin placed within a wooden coffin within a third, golden coffin. It was surrounded by buried food, furniture, dishes, clothing, games, and other everyday objects of the king's court. The two archeologists knew that the people of that time believed the spirit of the dead would awaken and require the ordinary materials of daily life. Here they found not only great wealth but a record of the customs and needs of an ancient people. The chamber walls were covered with pictures depicting the life of the royal court. There were scenes of battles and the hunt, all done in brilliant colors and with perfection of detail. They found, too, curious pieces of furniture, showing lions, crocodiles, and other African animals. Carter and Lord Carnarvon realized that they had unveiled a record of Egyptian life never seen before.

Before the year was over, they had loaded thirty-four packing cases of priceless material from the tomb along with four chariots and dozens of statues. These were loaded on flatcars and carried on a small railroad to the Nile River, where they could be placed on boats for the journey to Cairo. The mummy of the eighteen-year-old king was carried in its separate casing with its 143 pieces of jewelry. Carter filled thirty-three pages of his notebook with a list of the tomb's contents.

Today, historians know more about ancient Egypt because of this discovery, and people from all over the world may come to Cairo to see the splendors of King Tut and his times.

The answers for *Are You Really Listening?*:

1. 1922	9. 9 feet
2. November	10. furniture
3. 16	11. pictures
4. rubble	12. 34
5. Tut	13. 4
6. second	14. train
7. 18	15. 143
8. 3	16. Cairo

3 TEACHING PURPOSEFUL LISTENING

Most talk is informal, spontaneous, disorganized, and catch-as-catch-can. Listeners make sense of it by picking up specific items of information, by grasping the flow and drift of the message, and by intuiting the intentions and feelings of speakers. Teachers can help students become better at this kind of listening by giving guided practice in accurate listening, in listening for main ideas, in recognizing emotive language, and in critical listening in general. However, another kind of talk that is more formalized, structured, and purposeful is frequently found in schools, colleges, shops, laboratories, and offices. It is, fortunately, highly teachable. Student listeners with guided practice may become increasingly efficient at the skills needed to follow directions and understand structured presentations. Teachers can teach such key skills as recognizing a speaker's intent, following sequence, noting structure, recognizing specific patterns of organizations, and picking out signal words and phrases. Here is an area of the listening program where students may immediately profit by learning those listening skills most needed for success in school, work, and later life.

This chapter examines two important types of *purposeful listening:* listening to follow spoken directions and listening to recognize the organization of spoken discourse.

Following Spoken Directions

The skill of following a speaker's directions is probably a composite of several subskills, such as recognizing the speaker's intent, defining one's own purpose for listening, noting details, distinguishing between relevant and irrelevant details, and following sequence. Fortunately, all these subskills are teachable and improve with practice.

Ideas are presented for helping students in middle school, junior high, and high school, as well as ideas for correlating listening skills with other language arts and the other content fields.

Teaching Ideas for Middle School and Junior High

Some of the following strategies grow out of earlier instruction in accurate listening; some are planned to help students become conscious of the value of following spoken directions carefully.

1. Discuss with students the importance of following directions by asking such questions as:

   Where do people have to follow directions?
   Why is this an important skill in school? on the job?
   Who, in particular, would have to be a good listener to directions? Why?
   Why is following directions difficult for the average person?
   What are the problems a listener encounters?
   When did you last have to follow spoken directions? What problems did you have?

2. Try a simple warm-up game such as this version of Simon Says done with eyes closed:

   Put your right thumb on your left ear lobe.
   Place your left hand on top of your right thumb.
   Put both hands flat on the desk top.
   Raise only your left thumb.
   Grip your left thumb with your entire right hand.

3. Point out that games like Simon Says are easy but involve many of the same skills needed in real-life listening situations. Students can act out the following situation to demonstrate the necessity of accurate listening when following spoken directions:

   You are planting seeds and cannot hold the package while you work, so a friend reads the directions aloud to you. "Loosen the soil to a fine condition. Cover each seed with a quarter inch of fine soil. Plant each at least five inches apart. Make each row eighteen inches apart."

4. Point out that memory plays a part in following directions. Read the following situations and allow students to test themselves on their ability to recall the necessary information.

For a free copy of Mr. Harris's talk, send your name and address to Educational Services, General Motors Corporation, Box 364, Detroit, Michigan 78965.

> What is the box number?
> What will you get?
> What city do you send to?
> What was the zip code given?

A sample lesson will show you how pleasant and profitable it can be to study radio engineering at home. Send for free lessons now. No cost to you. No obligation. Write tonight to American School of Radio Engineering, 790 Commonwealth Avenue, Boston, Massachusetts 02215.

> What is being offered?
> What is the name of the school?
> What is the street number?
> How much does it cost?

When you hear the air-raid warning, follow these directions. Pull over to the side of the road. Leave lanes open for emergency vehicles. Shut off motor and lights. Open windows. Get out and go to a shelter if one is available. If not, crouch down in the car. Resume travel only when the all-clear sounds. For official civilian defense instructions, tune to the designated emergency broadcast radio station.

> Should you remain in your car?
> Should you open or close your windows?
> Which lane should you stay in?
> Should you turn off the car lights?
> What radio station should you listen to?

Because tomorrow's assembly is scheduled for fourth period, girls in sections 3–G, 3–K, and 3–M will eat during the second lunch period. Boys in these sections will report to the assembly hall at the end of the first lunch period.

> Which students are to have second lunch?
> When should girls report?
> Where should the boys go?
> When should they go?

Walk east on Common Street for two blocks until you come to Lynch's Drugstore. Turn right and continue on Madison Street. Number 264 Madison Street is the third house from the corner of Madison and Common Streets.

> How many blocks must you walk before you reach the drugstore?
> How many houses from the corner is the one you want?
> What is the number of the house?
> What is the name of the drugstore?

5. Give students practice in responding on paper to spoken directions.

Listen to these directions. Do not write until I have finished.

a. Make an *X* on the third line from the top of the paper. Make three zeros on the sixth line from the top. Draw a line connecting the *X* with the middle zero.

b. Draw a triangle with three equal sides. Label angles of triangle *A*, *B*, and *C*, beginning at lower left angle. Draw a line from *A* to a point midway between *B* and *C*.

c. On your paper write every other letter in your first and last names. Begin with the second letter of your first name. Put a circle around every vowel you write. Draw a straight line above every consonant.

d. On your paper write the odd numbers from 1 to 11 in a row. Begin with 1 and end with 11. Subtract the smallest number in this series from the largest. Write the answer under the last number in the series.

e. In the row of numbers you have written, multiply the third number from the left by the next-to-the-last number. Write the answer under your answer to number 4.

f. When I have finished, you will be asked to draw a rough map showing the following: To go from town A to town B, drive east on Main Street as far as the intersection of Main and River Streets, about one fourth of the distance. Turn left on River Street and continue for a short distance until you come to Route 1. Cross Route 1 and continue on this road, which leads into town B.

g. When I have finished, you will be asked to draw a rough floor plan of the house I shall describe. Left and right directions are from the point of view of a person facing the house. Listen carefully. This house is L-shaped. Two rooms of equal size are at the front of the house. One room is in the rear wing. The outside door opens into the room at the right in front of the house. There are two windows to the left of the door in this room. The left front room has four windows, two in front, one at the side, one at the rear. There are three windows in the rear room, two on the left of the house, one on the right.

h. When I have finished, you will be asked to draw a rough diagram of this stage setting. Remember the directions for stage settings are given from the point of view of the actor facing the audience. Listen carefully. This is the interior of a mountain cabin. There is a fireplace at the right. A door at the rear leads outside. There is a small window to the right of this door. Another door in the left wall leads to a back room. The furniture consists of a bed between the outside door and the fireplace, a table in the center of the room, and three chairs.

6. Link direction following with content study. One literature teacher regularly has volunteers prepare large wall maps of Dorset, the territory described in Thomas Hardy's novels. When students read *Return of the Native*, they give directions from their seats about where characters from the novel went while listeners follow at the map the specific movements of the charac-

ters. This exercise is designed to enhance appreciation and understanding of the novel while providing practice in following spoken directions.

7. Try Ceiling Zero. Divide the class into two teams, each of which selects a controller, who must guide a fellow team member in for a landing on a night when visibility is zero. The pilot is blindfolded and, guided only by the spoken directions of the controller, must "land" in the front of the room. All furniture is moved against the walls, but to make the landing more difficult, members of the opposing team place such obstacles as books, overturned chairs, and lunch boxes in the way of the blindfolded pilot. This exercise leads to increased attention and provides good practice in following oral directions.

8. Set up useful learning situations. Have students serve as school guides. With the principal's cooperation, the class sets up an information desk in the school lobby each morning during homeroom period. When visitors and other students come in search of information, a student is ready with accurate spoken directions on how to locate the main office, the guidance office, the school custodian, and so forth. Students get practice in giving directions and must first try out their directions on other students. In addition to performing a useful school service, students become more aware of the skills involved in giving and taking directions.

9. Move outside the school environment. Encourage students to prepare directions on reaching their homes. Volunteers give the directions, which selected volunteers try to follow. This activity works well when the school community is small and the teacher is able to supervise the volunteers.

10. Try recipe following. Invite someone from the home economics department to give the class oral directions on preparing fudge. Selected students then follow the directions exactly and make the fudge. The activity emphasizes the importance of notetaking and accuracy.

11. Give hands-on practice, too. Cut up colored construction paper into squares, triangles, rectangles, circles, and other shapes. Place five of each color and shape in an envelope for each student. Have students sit back to back in pairs.

Appoint one student in each pair the direction-giver and the other the direction-follower. The speaker builds a geometric design step by step, telling the other person exactly what each step consists of ("Put a yellow square in the middle of the desk. Put a red circle under it. Now place a blue triangle to the left of the circle."). The listener, unable to see the speaker and relying on oral directions, must reconstruct the same design during a set interval of time.

Teaching Ideas for High School

As noted in chapter two, many middle school and junior high ideas may be adapted for older adolescents. Specific ideas for high school classes are listed here.

1. Spend time discussing the importance of following directions, both in school and on the job. Ask students to list occasions when they have had to follow spoken directions in the past and occasions in the future when they will be required to be careful listeners. Point out the need for them to listen to items in sequence in school assignments, on their part-time and summer jobs, and in their homes. Focus particularly on questions such as: What are obstacles for listeners? How can such obstacles be surmounted? How can the average person learn to follow spoken directions better?

2. Take assignments from content-area teachers to use in listening sessions. For example, "Here is a typical science assignment. Listen carefully. I'll read it only once. Be prepared when I'm through to repeat the main steps, the exact order, and the final task. Think of problems listeners might run into when following these directions. How might you change them for the better?"

3. Have students give directions to one another. Some possible topics are putting on a suit jacket, replacing laces in gym shoes, or tying a necktie. The students who volunteer to follow the directions must do exactly what the speaker tells them to do.

4. Encourage students to collect examples from everyday life: "What's the last time someone gave you directions outside of school? Write these down as you remember them, and we'll

try them out on one another." Often the examples students bring in from their jobs and homes provide excellent materials for practice sessions.

5. Have students create their own paper-and-pencil exercises. Share with classes the exercises listed previously under *Teaching Ideas for Middle School and Junior High.* Encourage students to develop similar exercises that may be tried out on other students.

6. Have volunteers prepare in advance detailed instructions for completing an activity in class (such as drawing a musical staff with the first notes of a popular song or a map of the speaker's neighborhood). Listeners follow directions as given and share the results afterward with the speaker. Questions for discussion are "What went wrong? Was it the speaker's fault or the listener's?"

7. To help students be aware of sequence, list on the chalkboard before a talk the five main points—out of order. Tell students to listen carefully and place the items in what they think is proper order. Allow time afterward for discussion of the importance of correct sequencing in giving and following directions.

Correlating with Other School Subjects

The listening skill of following spoken directions neatly correlates with related skills in speaking, reading, and writing and with other content areas. One example is an assignment revolving around the topic of changing crankcase oil. First, it is a speaking lesson in which students must decide the main points they want to get across, the logical order of presentation, the appropriate transition words, and the possible difficulties listeners may encounter. Volunteers then try out their spoken directions on other volunteers who actually do the oil changing in the school shop. Listeners keep a record of difficulties they encountered in following directions. Next, both speakers and listeners together write out the directions, edit their work, duplicate it, and present it to the entire class as part of the teacher's lesson in following directions in reading. As the teacher points out, similar cognitive processes underlie giving and taking directions in all contexts —reading, writing, speaking, and listening. There-

fore, correlating instruction in all four skill areas enhances learning. Other teachers approach the basic skill of following directions in English class and in other content areas by using such writing tasks as preparing a manual for bicycle repairs; developing cookbooks; producing classroom guides for the shop, science labs, or home economics kitchens; and preparing all varieties of how-to-do-it manuals. The writing tasks are usually preceded by speaking-listening "tryouts" and followed by reading activities based on the students' written directions.

Implicit in all such instruction is attention to transition words and phrases or "signal words." As students prepare to give or write out directions, they should be shown that speakers and writers signal their intentions by using such terms as *first, second, next,* and *finally.* Good listeners—and readers, too—are able to use these signals to follow the sequence and discriminate among items. Teachers may make clear the value of recognizing transition expressions by (1) listing them on the board, (2) duplicating common ones for student notebooks, (3) having students locate transitions on printed direction sheets, (4) encouraging students to use transitions as they write out directions, and (5) providing practice sessions for students to jot down transitions in aural-oral situations.

Recognizing a Speaker's Plan

Much of the listening performed by students in school and college (and often as they listen to radio and television announcements and speeches) is based upon *structured discourse.* The speaker has planned and organized the talk. The presentation has a beginning, a middle, and an end. It rests upon some design the speaker has consciously (or sometimes unconsciously) selected.

Even a modicum of instruction may have a dramatic effect upon the listener's ability to profit from such material. When listeners "see" the speaker's organizational plan, they are better able to sense the intent and direction of the talk. Cognitive psychologists, especially those interested in schema theory, say that comprehension is enormously improved when the speaker's (or writer's) schema or organizational pattern is perceived by the listener (or reader).

What Are the Basic Patterns?

Many years ago, reading specialists noted five patterns that seemed to underlie the writing in most school textbooks. These same patterns are frequently found in spoken presentations.

Simple enumeration. Here the speaker notes that several items will follow in some sequence. A history teacher may say, "Six traits distinguished the early Spanish settlers from other settlers." Listeners should be immediately alerted that a list will probably be presented. A science teacher says, "There are four points you should know before you begin this experiment." Students should recognize that an enumeration will surely follow. Speakers signal their use of this organizational plan by using such transitional expressions as *first, second, third, next,* or *finally.*

Generalization plus example. Good speakers support their generalizations with evidence. They know that it is not enough to say, "Americans in the Gilded Age ran wild after profits." Examples must be given to support this generalization. A literature teacher may say, "Hemingway reveals character through speech," but then must provide an example or two from a story. Trained listeners usually keep an ear open for evidence to support the speaker's generalizations, assertions, and inferences. Because so much formal (and sometimes spontaneous) talk is structured around this pattern, teachers need to give students much practice in recognizing supporting information in writing and in spoken language. Signal words here are *for example, for instance,* or *another example.* English teachers often link this listening skill to composition work by explaining that good writers "show instead of tell" and by demonstrating how topic sentences are supported by other sentences.

Time or sequence. College composition teachers frequently attack this same pattern in lessons on "process analysis" (the how-to-do-it theme). It is, of course, the pattern basic to direction giving and direction following, whether in speaking-listening or writing-reading. Time pattern is important in history, current events, science, and other content fields, but it is basic to most work in literature, especially the study of narrative poetry, fiction, and drama. The transition words and phrases associated with the chronological or sequence pattern are *first, second, next,* and *finally.*

Cause and effect. Here the speaker presents an effect and its possible cause or leads listeners from cause to effect. Most students need help in understanding the way speakers use and abuse this plan, but they can recognize it easily and learn to be wary. High school classes can learn to use the cause-and-effect pattern in their compositions and in preparing talks. Most student listeners can learn that certain transitions signal a cause or an effect. Common signals are *as a result, therefore, accordingly,* and *consequently.*

Comparison and contrast. This pattern allows the speaker (or writer) to explain one item more clearly by calling attention to the ways it resembles or is unlike an item already familiar to the listener. Good teachers frequently use comparison and contrast: "A noun clause is like a noun in that it does the job of a noun, but unlike a noun, it is a group of words with its own subject and predicate." History and science teachers regularly explain new concepts by noting how they are like and unlike concepts students already understand. Transition expressions associated with the comparison-contrast pattern include *however, nevertheless,* and *on the other hand.*

General Suggestions for Teaching Organizational Patterns

Many learning specialists and study-skills teachers believe that the study of organizational patterns should permeate all classes in all subjects. Listeners and readers are more effective when they perceive the structures underlying discourse. Speakers and writers do a better job when they know how to organize their material according to some plan. Many psychologists now believe that comprehension is enhanced when people are aware of the schemata around which information and ideas are organized. Listening teachers may improve instruction in pattern use and recognition in at least four ways.

Relate listening to reading and writing. When topic-sentence development is taught in composition class or main-idea sentences in a reading class, teachers may also review the generalization-plus-example pattern and provide additional practice in recognizing and using it in short listening exercises. All patterns may be approached—either at the same time or in parallel lessons—through reading, writing, and listening.

Help students visualize the patterns. Simple board drawings help students recognize patterns. For example, a bar containing a generalization can be supported visibly by blocks containing the necessary evidence. The time pattern may be expressed pictorially by a time line; comparison and contrast may be expressed by two side-by-side blocks separated by *but* or *on the other hand.* Such graphs and charts (at first made by the teacher and later by students) may be used in reading and writing class to guide students.

Give practice in testing organizational patterns. Once students recognize common patterns, present them with lists of topics (such as Hockey and Baseball, Setting Up a Bandstand, Mark Twain's Early Years, The Influence of the Beatles) and have them tell which pattern is appropriate for developing the topic in a talk or theme. Regularly share with classes tape recordings of radio and television talks so that students may discover the patterns speakers favor.

Teach transitional expressions. Because speakers tend to select certain transition words and phrases to connect the parts of their presentations, listeners who are aware of what they are doing can identify the structure and follow the movement of the talk. The list of key signal expressions in Figure 3 may

Key Signal Expressions	
Type:	Usually found in:
Example words for example for instance thus in other words as an illustration	generalization plus example (but may be found in enumeration and argumentation)
Time words first, second, third meanwhile next finally at last today, tomorrow, soon	narration, chronological patterns, directions (and whenever events or examples are presented in a time sequence)
Addition words in addition also furthermore moreover another example	enumeration, description, and sometimes in generalization plus example
Result words as a result so accordingly therefore thus	cause and effect
Contrast words however but in contrast on the other hand nevertheless	comparison and contrast (and whenever speaker makes a comparison or contrast in another pattern)

Figure 3. Key signal expressions.

be used in reading and writing lessons as well as listening lessons.

Spoken language includes many signaling devices that rarely appear in print. Remind students of the device used in the U.S. Navy to make sure that listeners are tuned in to the message: "Now hear this!" Give students examples culled from everyday talk around the school, such as: "Now this is important," "My main point is ___," "One thing I'd like to emphasize." Note that such expressions, often colloquial, serve the same purpose as the transition words and phrases encountered in more formal presentations: they call the listener's attention to specific parts of the talk. Speakers seem to use such devices automatically when they want to emphasize key points. They sense, too, that such signals assist their listeners in moving from one point to another. A follow-up activity for discussions of *Now-hear-this*-type signals is to have students search out similar items as they listen to other teachers, to speakers outside the school, and to people on radio and television.

Use frames. Less sophisticated students need guidance in listening to formal spoken presentations. They may know the basic patterns, but they are not yet ready to abstract the patterns. One effective approach for teachers is to provide printed frames. These are teacher-prepared guides that students complete during or after the talk.

A sample frame for a simple sequence looks like this:

1. The climax of the story you will hear is like the punch line of a joke. What is it?
2. What happened just before this?
3. What three events *had* to happen before the climax?
4. Complete the following story frame:

   Event 1: _____
   Event 2: _____
   Event 3: _____
   Climax or punch line: _____

A sample frame for a talk based on comparison and contrast looks like this:

_____ is different from _____ in many ways. One major difference is _____ . Another is _____ . Still another is _____ . However, they are alike in many ways. For instance, they both _____ . Also, they both _____ . Finally, they both _____ . A good title for this talk might be _____ .

A sample printed frame for a talk clearly based on the generalization-plus-examples model looks like this:

The speaker makes three main points. They are: _____ , _____ , and _____ . The first point is supported with two examples: _____ and _____ . The second point is supported by three examples: _____ , _____ , and _____ . Finally, the last point is supported with two examples: _____ and _____ .

Printed frames for longer lectures may include several varieties. The speaker may begin with an enumeration and follow it with three examples of cause-and-effect pattern. The lecture may then continue in a comparison-and-contrast pattern and conclude with another enumeration. For high school and college classes, printed frames may become increasingly elaborate. As many experienced lecturers have pointed out, however, the time spent in preparing and duplicating printed frames is well spent because such frame development forces lecturers to base their talks on a structure and to follow the plan in the classroom.

Notetaking and Study Guides

Listening with pen in hand is as important when listening to directions and to formal, organized talks as when listening for details. The notetaking listener listens more attentively and accurately not only to details but also to purpose and structure. A student practiced in simple notetaking habits not only catches and remembers more information and ideas from a spoken presentation but also tends to perceive a speaker's organization and to have a better understanding of the message. Many teachers have found that they need to build notetaking practice into their classroom presentations and that one good way to do this is with *listening study guides.* Such guides focus listener attention on the plan and details of the talk. Suggestions for developing and using listening study guides follow.

1. Outline the lecture carefully before presenting it. Duplicate the outline and make sure every student has one to follow during class. As the talk develops, call attention to main points and important details. Say: "In the next section, I am going to make an important generalization and support it with three pieces of evidence. As you listen, underline the generalization and, in

the space provided, fill in the evidence." To make students aware of transitional expressions, say: "On the outline only main ideas and supporting evidence appear. As I talk I'll naturally connect these with common transition words and phrases. In the left margin, jot down the transitions I happen to use as I talk." Allow time after the talk to discuss student responses: "What evidence did you fill in? What transitions did you write in the margin?"

2. Outline the lecture but duplicate an incomplete copy. After students have had practice with lecture outlines, have them fill in main headings or supporting evidence. At first, such outlined listening guides may be fairly complete; then after each session, more and more items may be excluded until eventually students outline the entire lecture. In a typical classroom talk, teachers may shift from one organizational pattern to another. Guides initially need to indicate such shifts: "Note that the first part of the lecture is simple enumeration; which organizational pattern is used in the second part, cause and effect or comparison and contrast?"

3. Tape-record appropriate radio or television speeches. Many television stations, for example, regularly present editorials and responses to editorials. These are short and usually well organized. They provide opportunities for students to listen to recognize organizational patterns, transitional devices, and speakers' purposes. Because they are tape-recorded in advance, the teacher can prepare listening guides for class practice.

4. Have other teachers record formal presentations for listening class. One English teacher has several of her colleagues tape eight- or ten-minute lectures for her classes. She (and sometimes the colleague) prepares guides for students to use as they listen. One of her guides looks like this:

a. What is the main topic of the talk? (to be answered *after* you have heard the entire tape)

b. What is the main point of the talk? (again, to be answered *after* you have heard the tape)

c. What organizational plan does the speaker follow—enumeration, time, cause and effect, comparison and contrast, or generalization plus example?

d. What transitional devices are used? (try to catch at least five)

e. When did the talk digress from the main point?

f. What information was given that was not relevant to the main point?

g. What is your personal reaction to the main point?

h. In what ways do you differ with the speaker?

5. Try the Cornell System developed by Walter Pauk for college students. He has listeners take notes of main ideas in a right-hand column of their notebook page during the lecture and afterward jot down key words and phrases in a smaller left-hand column, called the "recall" column. After class and when studying for exams, students cover the right-hand column with a piece of paper and try to reconstruct it in memory using only the cues in the recall column. The system works for college and high school students. It may be varied and simplified for middle school and junior high students.

6. Use listening guides as *advance organizers*. Recent research in learning theory indicates that when learners are given a preview of what they are going to learn *before* the learning experience, learning is significantly increased. Reading teachers sometimes give students a one-paragraph summary of the chapter they are to read; often the teachers provide an outline, a series of summary statements, questions to be answered while reading, or some pictorial representation of the main points. Listening teachers can do the same. A listening study guide may provide an overview of the lecture, its main ideas, notes about point of view, questions to be answered while listening, a summary of the message, and even a list of the transitional words and phrases.

7. Try second-chance lecture listening. When brief talks are taped and students follow them with a listening guide, opportunities for "retakes" or second-chance listening are readily available. Students listen to the lecture with their guides in front of them. They discuss what they have learned and compare notes. Then they repeat the tape and go through the experience again. Listening skills are sharpened, and students are more apt to master the lecture content.

8. Experiment with mapping. All students do not process incoming material in the same way.

For many, a sequenced outline is difficult to understand and use; and *all* material cannot be outlined. Much spoken material is spontaneous, informal, and discursive. Many teachers—especially in high school—introduce students to mapping as an alternative notetaking strategy.

After students have had experience with traditional outlining methods of notetaking, suggest that they simply write the key word in the middle of the page and that they then draw lines out from it to identify important subordinate points and additional lines from the important subordinate points to supporting examples and details. Try a brief, prepared lecture or a selected recorded talk that may be played several times. On the chalkboard, make a map along with the class, stopping the tape or lecture regularly to show students why certain lines "grow out" of certain points. Allow students opportunities to compare their maps with the teacher-made map and with other student work, noting that such notetaking maps are quite individual and personal.

A sample map of this chapter appears in Figure 4.

Sample Lesson Plans

One seventh-grade English teacher relates listening instruction to the other language arts through these lessons based on a mock television program called "Crazy Celebrities."

Objectives

To give students practice in writing directions
To give further practice in following oral directions

Procedures

1. Recall previous activities in following directions: "Why is it important to be able to follow spoken directions? What should a listener concentrate on especially?"
2. Encourage students to recall and discuss televised interview shows: "Which celebrities have you heard interviewed? Who did the interviewing? What kinds of questions usually are asked?"
3. Suggest an interview-to-end-all-interviews. Tell students to imagine an eccentric celebrity, one who has unusually odd views on every possible subject.

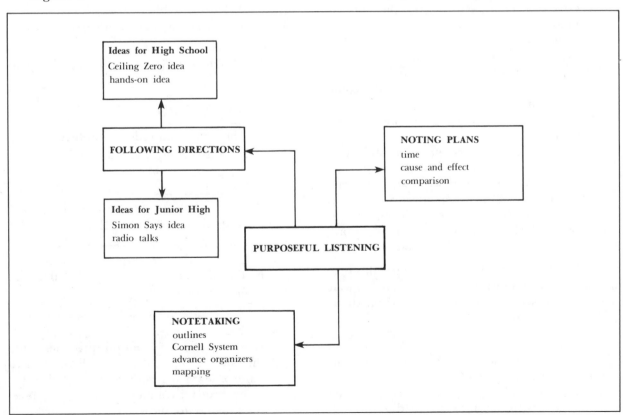

Figure 4. Sample notetaking map.

4. Have them jot down eight odd characteristics of their imagined celebrity and invent an equally odd name for the person.
5. Explain that the students should tell how their invented person might describe how to do something on a television interview. Say: "After asking some routine questions, the interviewer asks the guest to tell the studio audience how to do some simple task (such as putting on a sweater, tying shoelaces, locating a telephone number in the directory)."
6. Have students write out the directions that their crazy celebrity will give the audience. Suggest that they first write the directions in a straightforward sequence and then jumble the items so that directions will be difficult for a listener to follow.
7. Have students (working individually or in pairs) plan (1) the questions the interviewer will ask, (2) the answers from the guest, (3) a request from the interviewer for the guest to tell the audience how to do some simple job, and (4) the mixed-up directions given by the guest celebrity.
8. Give students time to practice their presentations.
9. Have three or four volunteers present their interviews to the "studio audience."
10. Have every student answer in writing the question: "Why are mixed-up directions mixed-up?"
11. Allow time for students to share their answers.
12. Lead the class to recognize that oral directions are frequently confusing because (1) the speaker fails to present the main items in the task, (2) items are given in incorrect order, (3) minor or irrelevant items are overemphasized, or (4) speakers may use words that listeners do not understand.

The ninth-grade teacher who developed this plan in following directions wanted students to be aware of the specific processes involved in direction giving and direction following.

Objectives

To give further practice in following directions
Specifically:
   in noting speaker's purpose in direction giving
   in identifying chief points in directions
   in noting and using transitions
   in distinguishing relevant from irrelevant items
   in noting and following a sequence of items

Procedures

1. Remind students of the difficulty of following oral directions.
2. Encourage them to list (in their notebooks or on the chalkboard) obstacles to successful listening in an oral situation.
3. Have each student choose one topic from the following list:
   finding the school supply room
   locating the school office
   finding the nearest fire station
   locating the closest hospital
   reaching a well-known local restaurant
4. Tell students: "You are standing in the door of the classroom when a stranger asks for directions. You have to give full and accurate directions, but you know how difficult it often is for a stranger to find his or her way around. Therefore, you want to give the problem some thought before you speak."
5. Have students think through their directions by completing this form:

   a. The purpose of these directions is
     ——————— .

   b. The chief landmarks or conspicuous places on the way are: ———————,
     ———————, ———————, and
     ——————— .

   c. The sequential order (from here to there) is to go from ——————— to
     ——————— to ——————— to
     ——————— .

   d. The actions or moves that the person needs to make are: ——————— ,
     ——————— , ——————— , and
     ——————— .

   e. The transition (or signal) words that connect these are: ———————,
     ——————— , ——————— , and
     ——————— .

6. Have students write out the directions using the form. (Remind them that they may need more or fewer spaces than the form gives.)
7. Allow time for volunteers to read their directions aloud to the class.
8. Encourage students in the class to discover

pitfalls and possible obstacles the stranger may encounter in following the directions as given.

9. Point out that this is a highly artificial situation but that the steps involved are usually found in all direction-giving and direction-following circumstances.

10. Suggest that students, as individuals or in small groups, develop a community (or school) guide in which points of local importance are listed with directions for reaching them from a central location. Such a guide may be duplicated for distribution in the community or school after a class editorial board checks directions for clarity and accuracy.

To prepare students to listen to college-level lectures, one tenth-grade teacher invited a colleague from a neighboring college to tape-record a psychology lecture.

Objective

To give students practice in recognizing common organizational patterns used in spoken discourse

Procedures

1. Remind students that formal lectures in high school and college are not always off the cuff. Tell them that experienced lecturers follow a structure that often includes the basic organizational plans they have studied: enumeration, generalization supported by examples, cause and effect, comparison and contrast, and time sequence.

2. Distribute copies of an incomplete outline of the lecture.

3. Explain that they will hear a ten-minute segment of a college lecture on long- and short-term memory given in a freshman-level psychology course.

4. Play the recording. Encourage students to listen with pen in hand.

5. When the tape is over, allow students time to discuss their responses. Note the speaker's basic pattern. Call attention to sections of the talk that include other organizational patterns.

6. Replay the recording while students double-check their outlines.

7. Allow further time for students to compare their responses with the recording.

8. Discuss the value of structure—both for the speaker and the listeners. Note reasons why speakers sometimes alter their lecture plan in the classroom ("Did today's speaker depart from the plan? Why? Did the speaker come back to it? Did you follow the plan? Why? Why not?").

Exercises

These exercises include four activities, two for following spoken directions and two for noting organizational patterns.

Giving and Following Directions

The chart in Figure 5 provides four geometric patterns. It may be used in a variety of ways. For example, a volunteer may come to the chalkboard without a copy of the chart and try to reproduce it following only the spoken directions of another volunteer (while others in the class follow along with their charts before them). All four patterns may be used in a single period-long activity or used one at a time four days in a row or four weeks in a row. When the four geometric patterns are familiar to students, volunteers may create similar examples for later class practice. The chart may also be used by individuals in pairs. The first student, viewing the chart, gives directions orally to another who has only a blank sheet of paper. The second must reproduce the pattern by following the spoken directions. In a second round, the second student tells the first how to draw the figure, but this time the second has the chart open and the first now has the blank paper. Again, after students become familiar with the four drawings, they may create similar figures and continue such practice sessions.

Following Spoken Directions

The incomplete map in Figure 6 provides students with a rough sketch of a neighborhood. Using it as a guide, listeners must develop a detailed map from spoken directions heard only on the telephone. Have the teacher or a student volunteer tape-record the following set of directions. When the recording is played, student listeners fill in street names and important places. Afterward, they may compare their maps for accuracy and listen again to the tape recording to double-check the details.

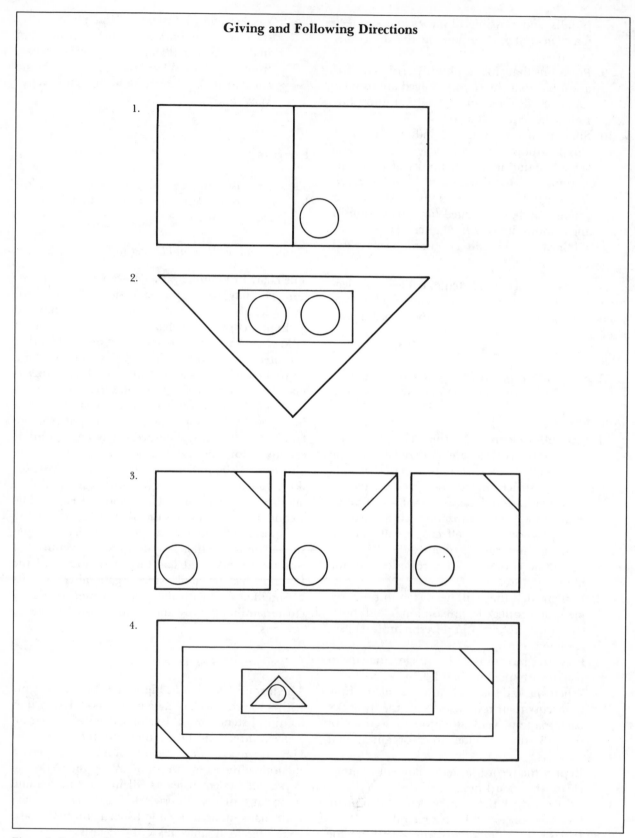

Figure 5. Exercise sheet for Giving and Following Directions.

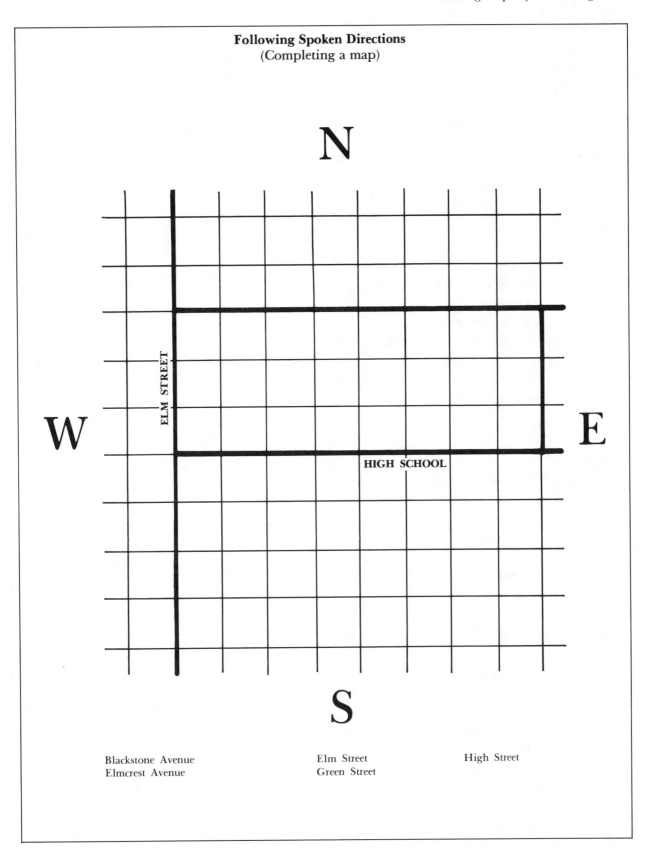

Figure 6. Exercise sheet for Following Spoken Directions.

Noting Organizational Patterns

Talk #1

Check the organizational plan the speaker uses

_____ Simple enumeration

_____ Cause and effect

_____ Comparison and contrast

_____ Time or sequence

_____ Generalization plus example

List the transitional expressions:

Talk #2

Check the organizational plan the speaker uses

_____ Simple enumeration

_____ Cause and effect

_____ Comparison and contrast

_____ Time or sequence

_____ Generalization plus example

List the transitional expressions:

Talk #3

Check the organizational plan the speaker uses

_____ Simple enumeration

_____ Cause and effect

_____ Comparison and contrast

_____ Time or sequence

_____ Generalization plus example

List the transitional expressions:

Talk #4

Check the organizational plan the speaker uses

_____ Simple enumeration

_____ Cause and effect

_____ Comparison and contrast

_____ Time or sequence

_____ Generalization plus example

List the transitional expressions:

Figure 7. Exercise sheet for Noting Organizational Patterns.

The All-purpose Listening Study Guide

Use this guide as you listen to spoken presentations in class. When you have become familiar with it, you may wish to create your own personal listening study guide.

1. What is the general subject of this talk?

2. What is the specific occasion? (Give name of class, speaker's name, and date.)

3. What is the chief point or main message? (This may be answered *after* the talk is over.)

4. What organizational plan does the speaker follow? (Is it enumeration? comparison and contrast? cause and effect? generalization plus examples? a time or sequence pattern? Is it a mixture of patterns? Which are used?)

5. What transitional expressions does the speaker use?

6. Does the speaker digress from the main point?

7. In what ways do you differ with the speaker?

8. What interested you the most? the least?

9. What is your personal reaction to the main point of the talk?

10. Write the speaker's main point in no more than three sentences.

Figure 8. All-purpose listening study guide.

Voice on telephone: The main highway along the top of the map is Blackstone Avenue. It is north of the city. To reach Elmcrest Avenue where the concert is taking place, drive south along Elm Street five blocks. Then go east on Green Street for eight blocks. You will see a high school on Green Street across from a Mobil station. After going eight blocks along Green Street, turn south on High Street; then go down High Street four blocks to a large bank building and turn west. This is Elmcrest. The concert is in an auditorium also used for sports events. It is three streets west on Elmcrest.

Before students listen to the recorded directions, they should be told to pencil in all the streets and avenues named by the voice on the telephone because someone else will need the map and directions. The incomplete map given lists all street and avenue names on the bottom so listeners can spell each one correctly. After students have listened to the directions once and have made and compared their maps, they may listen to the recorded voice again to double-check their results for accuracy.

Noting Organizational Patterns

Once students have reviewed the basic organizational patterns speakers often use, the following four talks may be read aloud to them. Their job is to indicate on the exercise sheet the type of pattern and the transitional expressions the speaker uses. The talks may be read directly by the teacher, tape-recorded by the teacher, or read and taped by a student volunteer. Figure 7, the exercise sheet for Noting Organizational Patterns, may be used over again during the school year with other short talks that teachers or students may locate or create.

Talk #1

Changing a ribbon on an old portable typewriter can be murder. First, you need to pry open the top of the machine. Then take out the old ribbon. As you do it, you need to watch and make sure you remember exactly how the old ribbon fitted in. Take the old ribbon to the store with you because sometimes you can't go by the name on the typewriter. Show it to the person in the store and get the same kind if possible. You need to unravel the new ribbon and fit the end into the old spool. Next, you try to get the new ribbon back in the same route the old one came out of! Finally, you put the top back on and see if the machine works. If it doesn't, you start all over again and hope for the best.

Talk #2

There are dozens of reasons to explain why we have inflation. I'm going to focus on just a few. First, we are the victims of the oil-producing countries. They have decided that they have a monopoly on oil and that they should get as much money as they can from the countries that do not produce oil. Second, too many of our government pension plans are tied into the inflation rate. That means that when the cost of living rises, the pension plans, like Social Security and veterans' benefits, go up too. Third, there is government spending. As long as the state and federal governments spend and spend, inflation increases. Finally, there is greed. One businessman sees that costs are rising, so he just charges more and more.

Talk #3

Miss Harrower is the most egocentric person I know. She never, for example, lets you tell about your interests without turning the conversation around so that she can tell about what interests her. From the time she starts to talk until she ends, she gives you story after story about herself and how life is treating *her*. To give just another example, I'd say that she can turn the most general discussion into a long lecture on what *she* thinks, what *she* wants, what *she* believes. For instance, the last time I talked to her, I never got a chance to tell her a thing: she monopolized the whole conversation and told me what she did during vacation, what she was going to do during the next vacation, and what was wrong with vacations in general!

Talk #4

Stan and Harry have a lot in common, but boy are they different! Both play the guitar, but Stan worships Jimi Hendrix while Harry likes Segovia. They both spend all their time practicing, but Stan copies records and Harry plays from scores. Stan relies on what he calls "musical feelings," while Harry, on the other hand, trusts his teacher's judgments about music. To me, Stan is an intuitive player in contrast to Harry, who is "schooled." Both are great, and I think they'll go places.

The All-purpose Listening Study Guide

Ideally, teachers should prepare listening study guides for formal spoken presentations—occasionally, if not frequently. For important lectures, teachers should give each student listener a guide to use in following the talk that includes an advance organizer, questions, and an outline. The all-purpose guide presented in Figure 8 is designed to fill a gap: students should be able to carry it to all lecture classes, use it, elaborate on it, and make it a part of their personal study equipment. Before distributing copies to students, teachers should review many of the points discussed in chapter three.

4 TEACHING CRITICAL LISTENING

Since language arts teachers first became interested in listening, many have singled out *critical listening* for attention. Since so much of what children, adolescents, and adults know is based upon information and ideas taken in by the ear, many teachers decided that they should help students better examine the ways in which such information is acquired. The ubiquity of television, radio, and motion pictures in American society and the time spent by students with these media support the belief that Americans learn more about life through their ears than they do in the formal structure of the American school room. Ask many students, "How do you happen to know *that*?" and they will say, "I heard it on the radio," or "I heard it on TV." Information about their local communities, national politics, the world situation, economic concepts, political ideals, ethical standards, attitudes toward marriage and the family, habits of food selection and nutrition, even understanding of human motivation—all are increasingly left in our society to the tutelage of radio, television, and films.

In a democratic society where freedom of speech assures equal rights to the honest advocate and the demagogue, critical listening becomes a matter of major importance. It is possible for skillful but unprincipled speakers to address enormous audiences. They are now in a position to shape public opinion, influence voters, and affect behavior. And listeners can be bombarded with spoken information that they have little skill in criticizing before they assimilate it.

Can teachers help students scrutinize spoken language more effectively? Can they teach young people to be better critical listeners? Because of research and practice in critical listening instruction in the past decades, it is possible to give positive answers to both questions. The next pages present a variety of classroom-tested ideas for teaching key skills in this area.

Key Critical Listening Skills

Five important critical listening skills are presented here with suggestions for the classroom.

Recognizing emotive language. Some language is, by its nature, objective and relatively free from emotional overtones. Other language, by design or chance, is emotive. Uncritical listeners too often fail to distinguish between the extremes. Even adult listeners sometimes do not realize that speakers are deliberately trying to arouse their feelings. A first step in improving students' ability to listen critically is to show them something of the nature of emotive language.

Start by demonstrating to students the emotive power of words. Some teachers do this with individual words, such as *love, mother, America, God, communism*. Others show students examples of good emotive language at work—in poetry, in political documents, in the Pledge of Allegiance. Students may be led to see that perfectly ordinary words in daily use do indeed carry emotional overtones. Follow-up activities to such demonstrations often have students collect from their own immediate environments words that trigger feelings. (Teachers may or may not choose to deal with curses or profanity, although the emotive power of such words should at least be mentioned in upper-level classes.)

A second step is to contrast clear-cut examples of straight report language with powerful emotive language. Some teachers start simply with paired statements, one of which is full of "loaded" words and the other unemotional:

> The criminal is charged with two counts of armed robbery and one of assault.
> The man is in court today to answer some questions.

Many such examples may come from the ordinary discourse of students:

> Billy walked into the yard and took the bike.
> Billy sneaked into the yard and stole the bike.

Students may be shown that such words as *charged, armed, robbery, assault, sneaked,* and *stole* are emotionally charged and that these words tend to color the speaker's message. Once students begin to indicate an awareness of basic distinctions, they can be asked to collect examples from their own lives. Later, many students, especially those in the upper grades, can create paired examples to present to the class.

One teacher draws on the board a cartoon of a former girl friend, noting that the only neutral word to describe her is *overweight*. He then has the class offer positively loaded words that might describe her while she is still his friend. Once she rejects him for another, the class lists other synonyms to describe her. The two lists of synonyms usually look like this:

Positive Synonyms	Negative Synonyms
chubby	fat
plump	gross
voluptuous	lardy

The main point for the students to learn is that all the words more or less describe the same person. Each, however, carries different *emotional* overtones. (The same activity may be done with *underweight* and other common words.)

To link this understanding of emotive language to listening, many teachers bring tape recordings of ordinary language to class. As the recordings (usually based on dialogue from television dramas and situation comedies) are played, students are to jot down all words or phrases that they find emotive. After a few practice sessions, students begin to realize that some words are emotive to them and not to others but that many words in English carry emotional power to almost all listeners. The follow-up activities may include finding examples from ordinary school and home conversations and making up examples to share later.

Recognizing bias. Students in fifth and sixth grade may begin to see obvious examples of bias in radio and television commercials, in editorials, and even in ordinary speech. High school students should learn to detect bias in their sources of ideas and information. Teachers may begin with paired statements, such as:

Billy walked into the yard and took the bike.
Billy sneaked into the yard and stole the bike.

In previous discussions of emotive language, students have noted that *walked* and *took* are relatively neutral words, while *sneaked* and *stole* carry strong emotional overtones. They may begin to realize at this point that the two speakers, either deliberately or unconsciously, selected words that reveal their own attitudes toward Billy and that encourage listeners to share their attitudes. Recognizing a speaker's (or writer's) bias initially may present some teaching difficulties, but even in lower grades students learn the skill with practice.

One way to help students see ways in which word choice indicates speaker bias is to present jumbled lists, such as the one below, and have students place words into columns labeled *Favorable, Unfavorable,* and *Neutral:*

venerable, old, antiquated
time-tested, old, outmoded
progressive, modern, radical
community, people, mob
strong man, absolute ruler, dictator

Ask: "Who is apt to call an idea 'time-tested'—the speaker who is in favor of it or the one who is against it? What might the speaker who is against the idea call it? Who might refer to an old man as 'venerable'—his admirers or his enemies? How does a speaker's choice of words indicate a certain attitude toward a person or idea? What examples can you recall of speakers revealing their personal bias by their words?

To help students better understand the effect of word choice in critical listening, place these three expressions on the chalkboard:

go-getter salesman
energetic salesman
high-pressure salesman

Explain that Charley, "our friendly neighborhood used-car dealer," has sold many cars in his time, some excellent vehicles and some clunkers. All his customers are impressed by his nonstop oral presentations, but the satisfied customers can usually be recognized from the unsatisfied ones. Ask: "What are the satisfied customers apt to call him? What expression will probably be used by those who purchased the clunkers?"

Have students neutralize popular television advertisements. Bring into class transcriptions of ads heard regularly on programs that students tend to watch. Note that these ads are prepared by people biased in favor of the product and contain emotionally loaded words. Have students listen to the ads to identify the loaded words and then rewrite the same ads substituting relatively neutral words.

Present students with printed copies of two news reports:

The State Department official courageously maintained innocence.

The State Department official refused to admit guilt.

Ask: "Which news report is biased against the official? What words and expressions reveal the bias?" (Such questions may lead into discussions of the purpose and responsibilities of newscasters and analysis of points of view on network news.)

Encourage students to prepare radio newscasts or editorials that are deliberately biased. These may then be tested out on the class to see if other students recognize the bias and note the words that give it away.

Distinguishing between fact and opinion. Sometimes speakers share factual statements (that is, statements that may be verified by others); sometimes they present their own personal opinions under the guise of fact. Explain the distinction to students by contrasting such comments as:

That new kid was picked up by the cops once.
The new kid is a regular juvenile delinquent.

Note that the first statement may be checked (the youth was or was not picked up by the police), but the second statement, as it stands, is the judgment or opinion of the speaker. Students should learn the danger listeners face when they accept opinions as facts. Facts may be correct or incorrect; opinions are simply reflections of how the speaker *feels*.

Present the class with a series of paired comments such as these:

Bob has been tardy for school three times this month.
Bob is a lazy loafer.
Susan got straight *A*'s in math all year.
Susan is a mathematical genius.
Debbie could play the piano when she was four.
Debbie is a musical whiz.

Students should recognize that opinion statements are important: they express a speaker's opinion and may be correct. The danger is that listeners will confuse a speaker's personal judgment with factual evidence; the speaker may be basing an opinion on inadequate evidence.

Present students with several opinions and have them show the kinds of factual statements needed to support them. Some possibilities include:

Speaker's opinion: Mrs. Jones is very religious.
Possible factual support: She goes to church every day.

Speaker's opinion: He is a mean teacher.
Possible factual support: He makes kids do homework.

Speaker's opinion: Dave is bashful.
Possible factual support: His face gets red when he talks to girls.

Provide students with practice sessions in distinguishing fact from opinion. Start with three opinion statements and accompanying factual statements that might support the opinions:

Opinion: John is industrious.
Fact: John works in a supermarket after school every day.
Opinion: Ted is punctual.
Fact: Ted has not been late for school or work in five years.
Opinion: Joan is careless.
Fact: Joan lost both her textbook and bus ticket today.

Then, give students a list of opinion statements overheard in the teachers' lounge or cafeteria. Have them find at least one factual statement to support each opinion.

Jane is poised.
Jane is overly poised.
Bill is a good class president.
The lunchroom is too noisy.
My little brother is a nuisance.
Seniors are mean to freshmen.
Bill has a great musical talent.
Movies give a distorted picture of teenagers.
Television gives a distorted picture of family life.
Japanese cars are better made than American cars.

Share opinion statements from the news media and ask: "How would you support these opinions? What facts are needed to support the opinions? Are such facts provided? Are the opinions justified by the facts?" Some examples of opinion statements follow.

People have been eager to race cars since the day the world's second car was wheeled out.
We live in a time when workers are basically lazy.
Americans do everything more spectacularly than most people.
Of all sports, hockey is the most primitive.

Once students begin to distinguish fact from opinion, have them collect examples of unsupported opinion from radio and television. Suggest that they keep a log of samples with the source and date of each. Such opinions can serve as the basis of further class discussions.

Recognizing a speaker's inferences. Opinion statements are expressions of the speaker's opinion, sometimes based on facts, sometimes not. Inferences are "educated guesses" that speakers make based on the available facts; they may or may not be correct. The danger is that listeners will confuse inferential statements for facts. One way to explain this to students is to say:

> A strange man walks into our classroom. He stomps over to the window, looks outside, and says, "There are black clouds in the sky." He looks again and says, "It will rain soon." As he stomps out again, he mutters, "This place has lousy weather!"

Point out that the first statement is factual, because other observers can look out and check its truth or falsity. The last is clearly this one speaker's personal opinion. The second statement, however, is a special kind of statement called an *inference*. It is a guess or prediction about the future based upon the factual evidence at hand and upon the speaker's expertise in the field. If the mysterious classroom guest is familiar with the geographical area, an inference about the weather might be valid; if he is new to the territory, an inference is not much good. Remind students that listeners must be wary. Sometimes inferences, like opinions, are accepted as facts.

Present students with the following five sets of statements and have them label each statement either *I* for inference, *O* for opinion, or *F* for fact. Allow time afterward for students to share their responses.

1. I always received an *A* in my math classes.
   I received an *A* in algebra.
   I will do *A* work in tenth-grade geometry.
   I am a good math student.
2. Susan refused to go to the dance with me.
   Janet said she was busy when I asked her to go.
   I'll never get a date to the prom.
   I am not popular with girls.
3. Senator X voted against tax reform.
   He sends his children to private schools.
   He will never be elected president.
   He isn't very patriotic.
4. I am in tip-top condition.
   I haven't been ill since kindergarten.
   When I was four, I had the measles.
   I don't need health insurance.
5. It was over 90 degrees yesterday.
   It rained all day today.
   The weather will be terrible tomorrow.
   This part of the country has awful weather.

Collect inferences from media presentations and have students tell what factual evidence is needed to make the inferences valid. Some examples are:

Shop at X's and save!

Take Blubber's Pills and lose weight.
A vote for Sam W. Candidate is a vote for lower taxes.
A longer school year will save taxpayers money.
Eat sardines and prolong your life.

Encourage students to locate clear-cut inferences in advertisements for classroom analysis. Discussion questions may include: "Is it a prediction or guess? What factual statements are needed to support it? What credentials does the speaker offer to prove expertise in this area? In what ways does an inference differ from an opinion?"

Relate this critical listening skill to writing by having students develop brief themes containing the following five statements:

a statement of the writer's opinion
three factual statements that support the opinion
an inference that may be drawn from the facts

Have students prepare brief talks based upon the above outline. As each volunteer makes his or her presentation, student listeners answer the following questions on their outlines: Is it an opinion? Are these really facts? Is that a true inference?

Evaluating sources. Some speakers seem to know what they are talking about; others clearly are talking "from the top of their heads." Discuss the importance to listeners of ascertaining the credentials of speakers—especially when they speak about a controversial subject.

One way to introduce this skill is to give students a jumbled list of topics and "authorities" and have the students match the correct person with each topic. For example, one set of speakers may include Muhammad Ali, the name of the school science teacher, Bobby Orr, and the name of the school custodian; a set of corresponding topics would be repairing a fuse box, the roughness of NHL hockey, boxing in the future, and the world's worst volcano. Students can see that listeners expect certain speakers to be competent to speak on certain matters. As a follow-up activity, have students make up similar lists to try on the class.

Students may list the qualifications they would expect for a speaker on such topics as:

the future of the space program
televised high school courses
the history of rock music
guitar repair
the impact of televiewing on children
jogging

Students can develop guidelines for judging speakers. One high school class suggested several questions to answer about a speaker:

1. What are this speaker's qualifications?
2. Has the speaker wide experience in the field?
3. Who chose this speaker?
4. Is the speaker being paid?
5. Is there reason to suspect the speaker is biased?
6. Does the speaker have a hidden reason for discussing this topic?
7. Does the speaker expect us to *do* something? What?
8. Where may we find other opinions?

Warn students of the "they say" problem. Note that many listeners base their thinking upon information that does not come from a competent source. Some speakers introduce important information by saying, "They say," "It is reported," or "Research says." Encourage students to find examples of this habit and discuss in class the dangers of such *non-evaluation* of sources.

To show the dangers of hearsay evidence, type out a brief anecdote on a card. Take one student outside the room and read it aloud to the student. Have this student, in turn, take a second student outside to repeat (without the card) the same story. Have the second student repeat the story to a third, and continue through ten or more students. The last student who has listened to the story should tell it to the class, and all students should compare this version with the original anecdote, which the teacher hands out or writes on the chalkboard. Original and final versions rarely, if ever, agree.

Record a radio or television editorial or political speech. As students hear the recording in class, encourage them to follow along using a guide such as this:

1. Exactly who is speaking?
2. What are the speaker's credentials?
3. Are facts being presented? What are they?
4. Are opinions being presented? What are they?
5. Is the language emotive? Examples?
6. Are there loaded words? Examples?
7. Is the speaker making any inferences? Examples?
8. Does the speaker present hearsay evidence? Examples?

Such recordings may be played two or three times as students listen and check their guides point by point.

The Six Basic Propaganda Devices

In the years before World War II, social psychologists in the Institute for Propaganda Analysis identified the six basic tricks that propagandists regularly used. Since then, many teachers have introduced these devices to students as an approach to critical listening. The six are still used by advertisers, politicians, and other persuaders. Recognizing them still gives listeners an edge in the oral-aural marketplace. The basic six devices were given attention-catching names by the scholars at the institute. The original names are provided here with brief explanations of how each works and with some general suggestions for teaching students to be wary of them.

1. The Glittering Generality. Every item or incident may fit into *some* generality. Propagandists try to select for their purpose a generality so attractive that listeners will not challenge the speaker's real point. If the candidate for public office happens to be a mother, for example, the speaker may say, "Our civilization could not survive without mothers." The generalization is true, of course, and listeners may—if they are not careful—accept the candidate without asking such questions as: "Is she a mother? Is she a good mother? Does being a mother have anything to do with being a good candidate?"

2. The Testimonial. To persuade listeners to have strongly favorable feelings about some item, person, or event, the persuader links it with another that does have prestige and respect. To convice people to like a product, an advertiser associates it with a popular, well-liked athlete or film star: "Bozo Cereal must be good because Joe Footballstar eats it every morning." Students generally have had much experience with this particular propaganda device.

3. Name-Calling. Here the advertiser, propagandist, or persuader tries to pin a bad label on something listeners are to dislike so that it will automatically be rejected or condemned. In a discussion of health insurance, for example, an opponent may label the sponsor of a bill a socialist. Whether the sponsor is or is not a socialist does not matter to the name-caller; the purpose is to have any unpleasant associations of the name rub off on the victim.

4. Transfer. In this device, similar to the Testimonial, the persuader attempts to transfer the authority and prestige of some person or object to another person or object that will then be accepted. Good examples are found regularly in advertising: Miss Starlet-of-the-Year is seen using Super Soap, and viewers are sup-

posed to believe that they too may have healthy, youthful skin like the starlet's if they use the same soap. Likewise, politicians like to be seen with famous athletes or entertainers in hopes that the luster of the stars will rub off on them.

5. Plain Folks. Assuming that most listeners favor common, ordinary people (rather than elitist, stuffed shirts), many politicians like to assume the appearance of common folk. One candidate, who really went to Harvard and wore $400 suits, campaigned in clothes from J. C. Penney's and spoke backcountry dialect. "Look at me, folks," the candidate wanted to say, "I'm just a regular country boy like you; *I* wouldn't sell you a bill of goods!"

6. Card Stacking. In presenting an argument where the issues are complex, the unscrupulous persuader often chooses only those items that favor the positive side of an issue. Listeners get only the facts that support one point of view, and any unfavorable facts are suppressed.

Teaching the Propaganda Devices

This is one area of critical listening instruction that has been developed extensively through the years. Social studies teachers and English teachers, in particular, have prepared interesting and effective lessons to alert students to the tricks played upon them by propagandists. The following sequence of instructional steps has proved effective:

Explain the six propaganda devices
Give examples of each
Give students practice in recognizing each
Have students collect examples from their listening
Review the six devices regularly through the year

Some specific suggestions follow.

1. Encourage students to create advertisements for products they invent. Suggest that they first prepare a straightforward descriptive advertisement containing only accurate statements and then rewrite it as an unscrupulous advertiser might. Tell them to use loaded words, emotive language, opinion statements, and at least one propaganda device. When they share these with the class, other students have the responsibility of locating the tricks

of the trade and noting the specific propaganda device.

2. Initiate propaganda searches. After students have become adroit at finding specific devices on radio and television, suggest schoolwide or communitywide searches. Sometimes propaganda is heard in the most surprising places.

3. Have students *justify* propaganda. Explain that people who use the devices often can justify their activities. Ask: "When may it be acceptable to use propaganda? Is it ever acceptable to trick people? Have you ever used these devices? Can you predict a situation when you might want to?"

4. Suggest planning a political campaign. Have the class invent a fictitious candidate. In groups or individually, students work out the details of a nationwide advertising campaign, focusing on such questions as: "What qualities shall we emphasize? Which should we downplay? How can we use Transfer? the Testimonial? Plain Folks?" Volunteers may prepare television speeches, radio ads, and other talks for the candidate to present in different parts of the country.

5. As a group or individual activity, suggest that students analyze one hour of Saturday morning television. Remind them that the networks set aside each Saturday morning for children's shows and that many adults criticize these programs for their excessive commercialism. Have students draw up a chart indicating time by minutes and have them fill in time devoted to entertainment and time spent on commercials. Have them use the Persuasion Analysis Chart (given at the end of this chapter) to analyze one commercial and then note the particular propaganda device that may have been used in each of the others. Students who prepare the analysis should be allowed time to share their findings with the group.

6. Encourage interested students to write a children's show. Have them develop an idea for a thirty-minute program, prepare a script, and act it out with the aid of other students. They may make drawings of main characters if their show is to be animated. Each show should be designed to present one of the propaganda devices in action so that viewers learn to watch for it. If time allows, student productions may

be presented to the entire class or taken to a lower grade for presentation.

7. Remind students that one of the best ways to learn something is to teach it to others. Suggest that individual students or small groups prepare material to teach the propaganda devices to other students. They may prepare simple lesson plans and "play teacher" in another group, or they may develop lessons through comic strips, slide presentations, tape-recorded dramas, drawings, or even motion pictures. Explain that they must focus upon one particular propaganda device and find explanatory material that learners will understand. Such lessons may be displayed in the classroom or tried out on other classes.

8. Give students practice in noting the six devices by reading aloud examples of their use (or misuse) and having listeners indicate which type is found in each example.

a. Rocky Roll 'em Over, the heavyweight champion of the world, says: "Buy Hercules Boots because they are the best!" Which type of propaganda is this?

b. Senator Quagmire says: "Vote for me because I'll lower the tax rate, I'll build up military strength, and I'll make sure our police are adequately armed to fight lawbreakers." What device is being used?

c. Quagmire's foe says: "Vote for me because Quagmire is not a good American; the senator was a member of a subversive group for many years!" Which trick is this?

d. Another candidate says: "You should vote for me because I am a veteran of the last war, and everyone knows veterans are more patriotic than anyone else." Which of the six is used here?

e. Slugger Sullivan says: "In baseball, energy counts; that's why I recommend Nature's Own, the natural breakfast cereal. Eat it every day and you'll be sluggin' away like me!" Which trick is this?

f. Mayor Drizzle says: "Education is the safeguard of democracy. Vote for my ticket, and I'll see that the schools in our community are well financed." Which device is the mayor using?

g. Drizzle's opponent says: "I grew up in the ordinary neighborhoods of this town. I didn't go to a fancy private school as Drizzle did. I drive a nice Ford, not a big gas-guzzler like Drizzle. I understand your problems." How is this speaker trying to trick listeners?

h. Drizzle fights back: "My opponent is a socialist and would destroy all that's made our town great." What's Drizzle's device?

The Propaganda Detection Kit

One desired outcome of the study of critical listening and propaganda techniques is a "PDK" or Propaganda Detection Kit—*built into every student's ears.* Teachers of middle school and junior high students may modify the kit presented here and try to share an appropriate version with every student. High school teachers may have their students develop one on their own. In times when skillful speakers have ready access to the ears of all Americans—children, adolescents, and adults—it is clear that all listeners need some kind of PDK.

My Personal Propaganda Detection Kit

When listening to anyone, at any time, I need to continually ask:

1. What is the speaker's purpose? (Is the speaker just trying to pass the time? be friendly? Does the speaker have a reason for this talk? What is it?)

2. What are the speaker's credentials? (If the talk is social chitchat, it does not matter, but if the speaker has a definite reason for this talk, what is it? What is the stated or public purpose? What might be the hidden purposes?)

3. Is there evidence of bias? (Can I spot clues that give away possible bias? Is the evidence stacked? too carefully selected? Does the speaker's background give reason to believe a fair picture is being portrayed? Does the particular choice of words show prejudice?)

4. Does the speaker use emotive language? (Does the speaker favor loaded words? Are there pat phrases designed to trigger emotions? Is the rhythm, pacing, or style planned to arouse emotions? Is it the kind of talk where emotive language is acceptable —poetry, drama, ritualistic speech?)

5. Does the speaker make sweeping generalizations? unsupported inferences? (Do I hear predictions about the future without the speaker's reasons? Are these educated guesses or unsupported statements? Do I detect Glittering Generalities?)

6. Do opinions predominate the talk? (Are these opinions *only*? Are opinions balanced with facts? Is it the kind of talk where opinions are acceptable?)

7. Does the speaker use any propaganda devices? (Do I hear examples of Card Stacking? Plain Folks? Name-Calling? the Testimonial? Transfer? Glittering Generalities? If I do, need I worry?)

8. Do I accept the message? (Is this true according to what I already know? What reasons are persuading me? Am I being hoodwinked? Do I want to believe for emotional reasons? Am I biased? Do I believe this strongly enough to try to persuade others? Why?)

Can such a "kit" of questions be internalized? Social psychologists and, more recently, cognitive psychologists who have studied the techniques of persuasion say it can. Most listeners with practice can prepare themselves to listen critically. Is it the responsibility of teachers and schools to provide such instruction and practice? Most educators and social philosophers would say that it is. Unless students are given help in school, they will not receive listening instruction elsewhere in our society, and the evidence of history is that people who cannot listen critically may be victimized—as individuals and as a society. Time spent in class developing and helping students internalize their own personal propaganda detection kits is a step, however small, toward a more alert and safer society.

Sample Lesson Plans

One experienced ninth-grade listening teacher has prepared scripts that may be used in a variety of lessons in critical listening. The following can be adapted to fit different lesson purposes.

Objectives

To help students evaluate sources of information
To provide further practice in distinguishing fact from opinion
To give practice in recognizing speaker bias

Procedures

1. A few days before the lesson is scheduled, have selected volunteers prepare a tape recording of the following script. Tell them that they may (1) use their own voices, (2) ask adults with appropriate voices to read parts, and (3) make changes in the script if needed.

The Script

Narrator: We are going to listen in on a meeting of the Chamber of Commerce in a small country town. We hear the Chair first.

Chair: Ladies and gentlemen, the first order of business today is to examine the proposal for a rock festival in our town this July. Mr. George Smith has asked to address our meeting and tell you of his plan. Go ahead, Mr. Smith.

Mr. Smith: Thank you. My plan is this. You have an enormous field outside of town owned, I believe, by Thomas Todd, who has a farm down the road. He says he will rent it to me for a rock festival. The spot is perfect. There is a train station and a bus terminal nearby. The roads into town are excellent. I plan to hire several famous rock bands, and I'll advertise all over the state—newspapers, television, radio, the works. I'll charge a fee, of course, but I also plan to give 10 percent of what I get to any town charity you want. That's for your cooperation.

Woman committee member: I think this is a terrible idea! Shocking! This will turn into another Woodstock. Remember *that*? We'll have hippies all over town throwing beer cans and putting sleeping bags on everyone's lawn. It'll cause more work for the police.

Chair: Yes. That brings up a good point. What are your plans, Mr. Smith, for housing these thousands of people?

Mr. Smith: Well, I assume that a lot will stay at your local motels. That'll be very good, you know, for business here. Some will bring campers and tents, I suppose, but that will be good for business too because they will buy food here. And as the owner of the largest supermarket in town, Mr. Chair, you know that this is all money in your town's pockets.

Woman committee member: No. I'd never vote for this. The town just doesn't have enough space in the motels and parks. We only have a couple of restaurants. We'd be inviting trouble. And people like this are a bad influence. They drink. They dress in strange costumes.

Chair: Well, well. We ought to consider the plan. Whether you and I like this modern music isn't important. Rock is American music. Started right here in these wonderful United States of America. There's that to think about.

2. Have students write the numbers 1 to 10 in their listening notebooks and answer each of the following questions:

a. What was the general purpose of this meeting?

b. Why does Mr. Smith want to have a festival? (Point out that he never says *why* he wants it in specific language.)

c. How much profit does he propose to donate to charity?

d. Which charity will he donate money to?

e. Which speaker seems to have least to gain?

f. Which committee member has most to gain?

g. In what way will that speaker profit?

h. Which speaker is biased against rock music?

i. Which comments reveal the bias?

j. Which of the many statements you heard was a definite fact? Which was an opinion?

3. Allow students a second chance to listen to the recording.

4. Go over the questions and let students share their responses.

5. Lead students to realize that some speakers are biased, some are better sources of information on controversial subjects, and some offer opinions as if they were factual statements.

6. Ask students to identify words and phrases which typify emotive language. Ask: "When do speakers tend to use such language? Why would one of these speakers want to arouse listeners' emotions?"

7. Have listeners identify the speaker who tries to hide personal reasons under the guise of public-spirited ones.

8. Review the six propaganda devices and ask: "Which one is used in this discussion?"

One seventh-grade language arts teacher who regularly tries to link listening with reading and writing has students do variations of the following lesson.

Objectives

To give practice in distinguishing fact from opinion

To have students understand that well-formed opinions are based on fact

Procedures

1. Remind students of the difference between factual statements (which may be verified by another observer) and opinion statements (which express the feelings or beliefs of the speaker or writer). Present several examples of each and encourage students to recall and share examples.

2. Point out that some opinions may be acceptable to listeners because they are supported by factual evidence. Contrast:

a. "The show was terrible."

b. "The show was terrible. The actor who was supposed to be a young rancher was at least seventy years old. The plot was incredible: imagine having *747* jets in the

years after the Civil War. The settings were ridiculous: there are no ocean beaches in Kansas. And worst of all, they interrupted the program every five minutes with another commercial."

3. Point out that the opinion statements in 2b may be incorrect, but they are verifiable. Encourage students to apply the same opinion statement to a television show they have watched and then develop a speech in which the opinion is supported for listeners by three or four factual statements.

4. Have students write an opinion statement in their notebooks. Tell them that the opinion may be "good" or "silly" but that most listeners will heed it more if it is supported by facts. Have them write three or four factual statements underneath it to give the statement an air of authority.

5. Allow students an opportunity to share and discuss the results.

6. Suggest that each student find an opinion statement (on radio or television) that needs factual support. Have them bring it to the next class session for analysis and discussion.

A tenth-grade social studies teacher who believes critical listening and critical reading are "different sides of the same coin" includes this lesson in critical listening each year.

Objectives

To review basic critical listening-reading skills

To relate critical listening and critical reading

Procedures

1. Have students read a selected section from their textbook and answer the following questions:

a. Who is the author?

b. What is the author's background?

c. Where did the information come from?

d. Are these trustworthy sources of information?

e. Which statements are facts? opinions? inferences?

f. Is there indication of bias?

g. What is the date of the book?

h. Which information may be dated?

i. What other sources can verify this material?

j. What protection do readers have against misinformation and bias?

Persuasion Analysis Chart

Name of student conducting analysis:

Time shown:

Length of commercial:

Product being sold:

Reasons given for customers to buy:
1.
2.
3.

People included:

Description of action (if any):

Description of music (why selected, why appropriate, and if effective):

Description of scenery (why selected, why appropriate, and if effective):

Propaganda devices used:
1.
2.
3.

Noteworthy features:

Opinion of student conducting analysis:

Figure 9. Persuasion analysis chart.

Critical Listening Chart

Name of student conducting analysis:

Nature of spoken presentation:

Where heard:

Name of speaker:

Speaker's expressed purpose:

Speaker's possible hidden purpose:

Qualifications of speaker:

Examples of emotive language:

Evidence of bias:

Propaganda devices used:
1.
2.
3.

Examples of facts and opinions given in talk
Facts:

Opinions:

Noteworthy features of presentation:

Opinion of student conducting analysis:

In what ways was the talk effective? ineffective? Why?

Figure 10. Critical listening chart.

2. Allow an opportunity for students to share their responses to the questions.

3. Play a tape-recorded speech or editorial from radio or television and have students use the same ten questions to analyze it. Again, allow an opportunity to share and discuss responses.

4. Have students choose one of the following activities as a follow-up assignment:
   a. Write and record a speech for class analysis
   b. Record a speech or editorial from TV or radio for class analysis
   c. Apply the same guide questions to a section from a textbook in another course
   d. Tape-record a speech outside of school and bring it to class for group analysis
   e. Revise the ten guide questions as a simple and handy "Critical Listener's Pocket Guide"
   f. Prepare a brief talk for the class on "Why Everyone Needs to Be a Critical Listener"
   g. Plan a pep talk on the importance of critical listening that may be presented in a class of younger students
   h. Present such a talk and report back on its success

Exercises

The exercises for this chapter consist of two charts, the Persuasion Analysis Chart, which students may apply to radio and television commercials for a better understanding of the techniques of the professional persuader, and the more general Critical Listening Chart, which students may apply to most organized spoken presentations.

Persuasion Analysis Chart

It is suggested that enough copies of the chart in Figure 9 be duplicated for students to use on several occasions during the school year. The directions for students are to (1) select a commercial that appears regularly on television or radio, (2) follow it carefully one or two times before applying the analysis, (3) use the chart, and (4) bring observation data to class for sharing and discussion. Suggestions for teachers using the chart are (1) give classes enough introductory instruction so that students are familiar with the terms, (2) allow ample follow-up time for discussion of student findings, and (3) post or duplicate selected student charts so that classes will have a record of their observations and analyses.

Critical Listening Chart

Because this analysis guide (Figure 10) may be applied to many situations, teachers need to exercise care in assigning it. After students have had sufficient instruction in the skills and topics outlined in chapter four, teachers may ask students to apply the analysis to one of the teacher's own classroom talks. A next step may be its application to the talk of another teacher. However, this step should be taken only with the consent of the colleague. A third step may be the analysis of a tape-recorded talk taken from the radio or television. (As noted, station editorials and political speeches allow for appropriate analyses.) Students need time to discuss in class their observations and to link their findings with class lessons in critical listening. As in the use of the *Persuasion Analysis Chart*, selected student charts may be posted in the classroom or duplicated so that classes will have a record of their work.

5 DEVELOPING A SCHOOLWIDE PROGRAM

Specific activities, listening games, and other recommended strategies work for individual students, small groups, or entire classes. Students who have listened in the past with only "half an ear" may be taught to develop and use key listening skills. They can be taught to become sensitive, highly skilled listeners. However, unless programs are *schoolwide,* covering every student, every class, and every teacher, the danger always exists that some students in some classes may not benefit from a program, no matter how effective learning activities may be.

This chapter suggests a schoolwide scope and sequence of learning skills with notation indicating specifically when a skill may best be introduced, at what grade levels it may be retaught, and when it may be reviewed. The chapter also provides information on how teachers may test most effectively for success, using both standardized and teacher-made instruments.

Tips for Talking Teachers

Although most teachers in middle school, junior high, and high school are aware of the limitations of the lecture method, they continue to talk. "Yes," teachers say, "I know that I should have more small group work, more individualized learning projects, and more media in my classes, but it's easier to explain the material myself." These teachers are correct in many ways: talking is more direct, economical, and personal. If teacher talk and variations of the lecture method are here to stay (and surveys indicate that in most schools students spend more time listening to their teachers than doing anything else), then suggestions for improving teachers' oral presentations need to be shared by listening teachers with their colleagues in other content fields. Here are five specific suggestions.

Prepare students for what they are going to hear. Authors of the teacher's manuals accompanying basal readers have always cautioned reading teachers to build a background for the reading selection *before* children read it. They have advised teaching difficult or new words before boys and girls encountered them in the text, explaining difficult and new concepts in advance, and setting up a purpose for readers. In recent years, psychologists have advocated the use of advance organizers (summaries, outlines, or overviews that would give learners a notion of what they are expected to learn). Both research from learning theorists and decades of successful reading instruction reinforce the important point: students learn more when they have an idea, however vague, of what they are supposed to learn. Teachers need to remember this point. Too often, college lecturers and secondary school teachers present excellent material to listeners who are simply not prepared to take it in. To improve classroom listening, all teachers should:

1. Give listeners an overview (in the form of an outline, summary, or set of guide questions)
2. Explain new and difficult words in advance (by distributing a list with definitions and synonyms or by placing them on the chalkboard)
3. Explain new concepts in advance (assuming that listeners already know what in fact they do not know leads to major breakdowns in oral-aural communication)
4. Give listeners a purpose for listening (by noting, for example, that "I'm going to tell you the reason Thomas Hardy disguised his native country as Dorset")

Give students a listening guide. A well-constructed guide may include an advance organizer, a list of difficult words, explanations of new concepts, and guide questions. It can improve classroom listening in other ways: by forcing the teacher to structure the talk in advance of presentation, by giving listeners an outline to follow and perhaps complete as they listen, by showing student listeners that the talk is so important that the teacher went to all the trouble of preparing a guide, and by building into the lecture or talk instruction in note-taking. Ideas for developing guides and notetaking skills and a suggested All-purpose Listening Study Guide are presented in chapter three. Working from these, listening and content-area teachers may construct a variety of effective guides. One successful listening teacher has said, "If *every* teacher in the school would take the trouble to prepare a listening guide, learning would improve 100 percent!" As she likes to point out, "We talkers have a responsibility to maximize listening, because students are not naturally going to give it all they've got."

Insist upon listening with pen in hand. Because the human memory is a fragile dimension of mind and personality, people capture only a fraction of the spoken language that floats by them. And as noted in chapter two, they tend to capture and retain in memory mostly those items that for some reason touch them personally. The best justification for notetaking, then, may be that it forces the listener to decide what is important and to write it down. Successful listening teachers through the years have accepted the notion that some listening is for enjoyment and appreciation; listeners need not capture on paper *all* that they hear. But as these teachers would indicate, listening in school is mostly serious; it is intended to be captured and retained, and the best way to catch it and keep it is with a notebook. Thus, for formal presentations in class, teachers in all subject-matter areas should remind students continually of the importance of formal notetaking and insist that every student have and use a pen and notebook. Some strategies:

1. Give questions in advance (on the board or handed out) and remind listeners to listen for possible answers
2. Provide a rough outline for students to complete as they follow the lecture
3. Have students jot down "new-to-me" items (simple lists of facts or insights that the listener had not heard before)
4. Use a formal notetaking system (for example, the Cornell System devised by Walter Pauk, described in chapter three)
5. Provide maps, charts, or graphs that listeners may fill in only if they listen carefully (for example, one history teacher says, "In this talk, I'm going to make several comparisons of the populations of the United States and China over a period of a century; as I talk, keep track of the figures on the chart")

Personalize. Listeners pay attention to what touches them personally. Skillful speakers have always known this and have built into their talks bridges between the content and message and the listener. Good teachers, too, have instinctively done the same. They have realized that every time they include listeners directly in the talk, they have heightened involvement and have improved communication. At its lowest level, such personalizing has led to admonitions such as, "Sit up and pay attention, Thomas; you're to be tested on this." At its highest level, personalizing means incorporating the plans, lives, and aspirations of students into the topic. Personalizing may include:

1. Anecdotes about other students familiar to the class to illustrate key points ("This reminds me of the time Bob ran for class president")
2. Examples from the lives of students ("Inflation at the national level is very much like what happens to you when you can't accept a part-time job at a certain wage because the cost of gasoline to get to the job is more than the salary")
3. Examples from school events in the past ("The postwar election is similar to the student council election we had last year in that...")
4. Study guides directed at individual students (a Teacher-over-the-Shoulder guide, for example, includes the names of students in the particular class: "Bob, because you have experience organizing dances, you answer the question on page 78; Susan, because you know more than most people about golf, you can do the item on page 79 about terrain...")
5. Examples from the life of the teacher ("When I was in college, a similar thing happened to me")

One of the reasons research reports are difficult to read is that they tend to be impersonal. Objective, scholarly lectures are difficult to follow because they too are detached from the lives of listeners. Teacher-talkers who want to be listened to personalize their talks.

Give listeners something to look forward to. The most effective teacher-talkers build into their presentations goals to be anticipated. One popular college lecturer usually begins by hinting that he hopes no news reporters are present, implying that he has shocking material to share. His students listen attentively for his latest attack on the military-industrial complex, labor unions, or the administration of the university. Many teachers at every grade level have used the same technique. They note, "This question is sure to be on the big test," or "This item always turns up on SAT tests."

How can teachers build anticipation into their classroom talk? Several strategies have proven successful:

1. After giving the class background for the talk, ask students to list five questions that they want answered in the talk
2. After building background, tell students to listen in order make up test questions
3. Have students make predictions about the outcome of the talk ("What point do you think I'm leading up to?")
4. Stop when the talk is underway and have students jot down the conclusions they think you are aiming at
5. Stop in the middle of a talk and tell students to write down answers to specific questions ("If what I've said so far is true, what conclusion must we come to at the end of this presentation?")
6. Give listeners the actual test questions *before* the lecture, have them use the questions to structure their notetaking, and then base the content examination on the questions
7. Give specific tasks that may be completed only after hearing the oral presentation ("Here is a map of colonial Salem that you are to fill in for a home assignment; as I talk, make notes to help you later when you fill in the details")

Are speakers responsible for the extent and quality of listening? Many teachers say yes. A listening program that thrusts complete responsibility on the student listener, they would say, is simply not fair. Teachers have an obligation to prepare listeners, to provide study guides, to personalize, to give listeners something to anticipate, and to insist upon listening with pen in hand. Communication is, after all, a two-way street.

Testing for Success

Why test listening? Experienced teachers of listening suggest at least four reasons for testing listening skills.

1. A good standardized test of listening skills provides a means for schoolwide assessment and comparison with students in other schools throughout the country. It helps answer such questions as:
   a. How well do our students compare with other students at the same grade level in other communities?
   b. Do our students really need listening instruction in a formal program?
   c. In what general areas do they need help?
2. Teacher-made tests can focus upon specific skills. Standardized listening tests (like standardized reading tests) tend to examine general areas. Teachers need to know exactly which skills need to be developed. They need to know which specific skills students have already mastered. A good teacher-made listening test can answer questions such as:
   a. Do my students listen accurately?
   b. Can they follow spoken directions?
   c. Do they recognize a speaker's bias?
   d. Can my students see a speaker's plan of organization?
   e. Do they note transitional expressions?
3. Listening tests may be consciousness-raising devices. Many students are not aware of their listening abilities. A test—either teacher-made or standardized—may help make them realize the extent and quality of their own listening. It can help answer questions such as:
   a. How well am I listening?
   b. Do I need to improve my listening skills?
   c. What are my strengths? weaknesses?
4. Testing highlights the importance of listening in the school curriculum. Unlike reading, success or failure in listening is not readily observable. Listening tests may provide teachers and administrators with ways of seeing where they and their students have been, where they are now, and where they are headed. In the process, they help highlight listening instruction as a worthwhile, significant part of education. They can help answer such questions as:
   a. How well are students doing this year?
   b. Have they improved since last year?
   c. What areas need to be worked on in the future?

Standardized Tests in Listening

A few standardized tests in listening have been developed, and some are still available. One that has proved useful in comparing students with their peers across the country has been the Brown-Carlsen Listening Comprehension Test (originally published by World Book Company in 1955). This test was designed to measure immediate recall, following directions, recognizing transitions, recognizing word meanings, and lecture comprehension. Teachers who use it read aloud from a manual containing short selections and instruct students to respond to questions by filling in blanks on an answer sheet. Reliability coefficients for the test are high, and considerable evidence is offered in the manual to support its claims to validity. The Brown-Carlsen measure has been used extensively in research.

Another standardized test in this area is the so-called STEP Test, one of a series of achievement tests published originally by the Educational Testing Service in 1956. The Sequential Tests of Educational Progress: Listening Comprehension test was constructed to measure comprehending main ideas, remembering significant details, understanding the implications of ideas and details, and evaluating and applying material presented. It is also administered by an examiner reading aloud from selections in a manual as students check off appropriate answers on an answer sheet. Like the Brown-Carlsen measure, it claims validity and high reliability. Unlike it, the STEP Test measures students as young as fourth grade rather than just in high school and college. Both tests provide national norms and, although dated, are still useful in planning and evaluating a listening program.

Teacher-Made Listening Tests

Much more valuable for classroom teachers are instruments made by teachers for their own students. Five such tests are described here.

1. *Informal appraisals.* These are simple checklists that teachers keep for every student. One teacher duplicates these ten questions so that she has a page for each student in her notebook. She schedules an informal appraisal every two weeks, notes her answers to the questions, and dates each entry. A sample appraisal sheet appears in Figure 11.

Name of Student _____

Listening Behaviors and Habits	Dates Observed							
1. Does he/she get ready to listen?								
2. Does he/she keep attentive during oral presentation?								
3. Is less attention paid to fellow students than teacher?								
4. Does he/she look at speaker?								
5. Does his/her behavior show interest?								
6. Does he/she take notes?								
7. Do his/her class comments indicate a grasp of talk?								
8. Is he/she polite when the teacher talks?								
9. Is he/she polite when other students talk?								
10. Does he/she ask questions?								

Figure 11. A simple checklist for appraising listening skills of a student.

Such a device, this teacher says, serves as a reminder that *she* must be conscious of listening. It also reminds students that in her class listening is considered important.

A more specific instrument measures skills that a teacher has tried to develop. The teacher lists exact behaviors from the lesson plan or curriculum guide, duplicates them so that there is a copy for each student, and periodically checks for student mastery. A sample checklist measuring specific listening skills appears in Figure 12.

Such a checklist as this may be developed for specific skills in accurate listening, purposeful listening, noting a speaker's plan, or aspects of critical listening. Again, such a device reminds the teacher to watch for use of listening skills while reminding students that these skills are important to success in school and life.

A more general checklist for informal appraisal of an entire class may be constructed for a single area of listening. One teacher uses the list in Figure 13 for checking critical listening growth. A second informal checklist for appraising students' listening skills appears in Figure 14.

2. *Content checks.* In order to identify students who fail to pick up ideas and information in oral presentations, many teachers construct informal content checks. They select a passage from a textbook that students are currently reading (usually two to four pages from a chapter at the end of the book) and prepare approximately twenty multiple-choice questions based on content. They duplicate simple answer sheets listing the letters of the possible responses and distribute them to the class. Students are told that they are to take a test of listening ability: they need to listen carefully and then circle the letter of the correct response when they hear each question. Teachers can construct an ordinary tally sheet, estimate the average score for the class, and get a rough notion of how individual students listen in comparison to the class as a whole.

Some teachers refine such content checks so that they are able to measure growth in particular skills. For example, one teacher who uses such tests regularly during the school year has now built into the content tests items that measure such specific listening skills as "Recogniz-

Name of Student _____									
Observable Behaviors				Date Noted					
1. Is able to follow directions in a game such as Simon Says									
2. Is able to follow specific directions on a guide (such as, "Put an X on the second line from the top; draw a circle around the third letter of your last name.")									
3. Is able to draw a map by following spoken directions									
4. Is able to fold a piece of paper as instructed									
5. Is able to repeat directions for a specific task to a fellow student									

Figure 12. A checklist for appraising specific listening skills of a student.

Code: A Always U Usually S Seldom N Never Names of Students	Skills	Notes bias	Distin-guishes fact from opinion	Notes emotive language	Recognizes propaganda devices
1.					
2.					
3.					
4.					
5.					
6.					

Figure 13. A checklist for appraising critical listening growth of class members.

	Names of Students									
Observable Behaviors										
1. Had hearing checked with audiometer										
2. Has hearing loss										
3. Speaks too loudly										
4. Speaks too softly										
5. Leans forward when spoken to										
6. Has trouble following class discussions										
7. Has problems talking to other students										
8. Sometimes fails to respond										

Figure 14. A checklist for appraising listening skills of class members.

ing a speaker's plan of organization" or "Finding evidence to support a speaker's generalization." Sample questions sound like this:

Number 16. I am going to read four statements from the passage, labeled *A, B, C,* and *D.* Circle the one that best supports the following generalization.

Number 19. The passage followed a definite plan of organization. Circle *A* if it was enumeration, *B* if it was comparison and contrast, *C* if it was cause and effect, and *D* if it was a time sequence.

This teacher keeps an informal checklist of student names and scores, not only on tests to measure listening for details but also on specific skills. Constructing the latter type test is not easy, but it gives the teacher information that would otherwise be unknown.

3. *Taped tests.* Because of the work involved in constructing informal classroom tests, many teachers tape-record them. They too must build tests around textbook passages, prepare answer sheets, correct the papers, and record the scores. However, rather than read the passages aloud to the class, the teachers make recordings of the passages. The tape recordings may be used with several classes each year and may be kept from year to year. One aspect of taped testing is that it allows the teacher to sit on the side of the room and observe listening behaviors.

Some teachers have extended taped testing by recording outside their own classes. One teacher, for example, has a colleague in another department read a passage from a book used in that teacher's course, which helps students learn to transfer the listening skills acquired in English class to history, science, and mathematics. Another teacher records a friend's college freshman psychology lectures. She prepares twenty multiple-choice questions based on the lecture and tells her high school seniors that they are going to get a taste of college. The students take the test and discuss their answers. This sample lecture helps students to evaluate the listening skills needed in a real lecture situation. This same teacher uses the college lecture tape as the basis of lessons in notetaking and other varieties of listening with pen in hand.

Many listening teachers also prepare multiple-choice test items, answer sheets, and listening guides to accompany tape recordings. Students follow the talk using the guides to direct them to specific details and to the speaker's organizational plan. Tape-recorded tests may be used as assessment tools and as effective teaching devices. Students can listen to talks several times and begin to understand the specific skills needed for full comprehension of spoken language.

4. *Story tests.* Many teachers start with stories. Younger children have opportunities to listen to tales, narrative poems, and favorite stories; secondary students are frequently denied chances to sit and follow a well-told yarn. Listening class can provide an opportunity for adolescents to listen to narrative fiction—while providing their teachers with another chance to test and teach. Many high school teachers save appropriate short stories for end-of-the-day or end-of-the-week listening activities. They sometimes check the skill of following sequence or the skill of noting important details by asking six or eight questions after students have enjoyed listening to a story. One English teacher reads aloud a ten-minute story each Friday. As a simple (but effective) test of listening skill, she places ten details from the story on the chalkboard before she begins reading. When finished, she asks students to jot down the four details that are most important to the outcome. The collected answer sheets provide additional information about student listening ability, and the experience for students is relatively painless. A history teacher reads sections from novels and stories that relate to his course. Before he begins, he writes ten events from the story on the board in jumbled time order. As students listen, they are to rearrange the events in correct chronological order. In addition to enlivening the history course, the narratives give students valuable practice in listening for correct sequence.

Another English teacher carries story listening several steps further. She reminds her high school class that good authors reveal characters' inner qualities not only by direct statement but also by their speech and actions. After listening to an appropriate story, students write down three qualities of the main character and indicate the reasons for selecting these qualities. Students share their responses. Then the story is read a second time, and students listen for speeches and actions that reveal the character's special qualities. For example, in listening to Shirley Jackson's short story "After You, My Dear Alphonse," students may say the mother in the story is *prejudiced* or *middle class.* They must find specific speeches or actions that reveal this prejudice or middle-class behavior. (The mother, for example, speaks to the black boy as if he were a stereotypical inner-city boy; she corrects her son's grammatical usage in a way characteristic of suburban mothers.) Sometimes class discussions become so enthusiastic that students demand a second reading so that they can double-check one another's responses and reasoning. Lessons such as this provide for growth in listening skills and lead to increased understanding of basic literary concepts. "And," the teacher adds, "they have *fun* listening to the stories."

5. *Real-life situations.* Some listening teachers use real-life situations to test listening skills. One teacher has collected recordings of conversations in the school cafeteria, at school committee meetings, and in the teachers' lounge. With the permission of the speakers, she uses these recordings as the bases of informal listening tests. She prepares ten or twenty questions, has her class listen to the conversations, and uses the questions to discover how well students listen for details, follow sequence, detect bias, and perform other listening skills. The tapes then become the material for follow-up lessons and other learning activities.

Several teachers, cautious about recording actual conversations, write out conversations simulating oral-aural situations and have actors read the dialogue. One of these conversations is presented here.

Student's Voice: There is an automobile collision outside your house. You rush out to see what happened and overhear three people—a man, a woman, and a boy—talking to the police officers who have stopped at the scene of the accident. This is what you hear.

Man: That stupid idiot driver! She went right through the stop sign. I looked both ways. I thought she'd stop, but she plowed right through. She's half-blind anyway. Look at those crazy glasses she's wearing. And that silly hat. Those went out of style years ago.

Woman: Nonsense! I certainly stopped. I checked right and left. *He* zoomed down the street at eighty miles an hour. After I'd stopped for the stop sign, I began driving slowly through the intersection. That man is drunk.

Boy: The lady's car stopped. I saw it. She didn't come to a full stop though. The other car came out of nowhere. At least I didn't see him until the crash.

The questions to accompany this hypothetical conversation are designed to measure basic skills in accurate listening as well as purposeful and critical listening.

a. When did the accident take place?
1. as the boy walked down the street
2. while the boy was visiting his aunt
3. just before you came out of your house
4. as school closed

b. Which of these is a fact and not the speaker's opinion?
1. She's half-blind.
2. That man is drunk.
3. The driver's a stupid idiot.
4. The woman is wearing glasses.

c. Of all the people named, which one has the least to gain from the argument?
1. the man
2. the woman
3. the boy
4. the man's insurance agent

d. Here are four judgments that a listener might make after listening to these speakers. Which one seems most sensible to you?
1. One driver may have been injured.
2. One of the cars was wrecked.
3. There is a difference of opinion about who was at fault.
4. The police want to blame the man.

e. Which is a minor detail and not a main point of the argument?
1. One driver may have vision problems.
2. Someone went through a stop sign.
3. One driver may have been drunk.
4. One driver was dressed oddly.

f. To see how well you follow spoken directions, listen and do exactly as you are told. This will not be repeated.

Write the word *car* beside the number 2 in question *b*. Now draw a circle around the second letter of the word you have just written and make a line going from the circle to the number 4 in question *c*. When you have done that, write the third letter of your last name beside the number 1 in question *b*. Now draw a line from the second letter of your last name to the number 2 in question *a*.

Tests such as these take time: teachers must create the scripts, find people to read the parts, make up questions and answer keys, tape-record the scripts, and administer the tests. But many teachers feel that the time is well spent, because once the test is made, it is long-lived: "I spent hours making up ten simple tests," says one listening teacher, "but I've been using them for three years in many classes."

When to Teach What

Developing a successful schoolwide listening program includes:

1. Making all teachers in the school aware of the listening skills of students
2. Helping teachers speak in class so that listening is highlighted and maximized
3. Providing ready access to a rich variety of teaching ideas and strategies
4. Giving teachers a schoolwide scope and sequence of basic listening skills so that all involved in the program will know what to teach and when to teach and review

This chapter has suggested five specific ways in which individual teachers may improve oral-aural communication. These tips for teacher-talkers may be duplicated to share with the school faculty and may serve as the basis for an inservice workshop. It also suggested four reasons for schoolwide testing and numerous listening tests that teachers may use. Tests, whether standardized or designed by individual teachers, raise the listening consciousness level of both teachers and students and provide a means of assessment and diagnosis. The entire book offers suggestions for teaching activities.

However, teachers also need a structure on which to build the program, a framework that spells out the specific skills to be introduced, taught, and reviewed at each grade level. Such a scope and sequence in listening skills is presented in Figure 15. It may be modified for the needs and philosophy of a particular school. As presented here, it can serve as a useful tool and as the basis for valuable inservice workshops.

As noted in chapter one, not all experts in the field agree upon the specific skills or upon the sequence in which such skills may best be taught and learned. Some authorities in language arts question the skills approach to learning in general. However, the point of view taken in this book is that teachers need a jumping-off place, and a scope and sequence provides just that. The one presented

gives pegs on which to hang lessons. It also gives teachers involved in building a schoolwide program a structure for discussion in their planning sessions and a tool for bringing listening lessons into every classroom.

Getting a Program off the Ground

Listening *is* important. Mastery of basic listening skills is important to every student's success both in school and in life. Basic skills are identifiable, teachable, and testable. How may they best be developed schoolwide? What steps may individual teachers, supervisors, and administrators take to initiate a listening program that truly touches every student in the school?

The Need for a Schoolwide Program

Individual teachers in individual classrooms across the nation have taught basic skills in listening. Since language arts specialists and various local, regional, and national professional organizations began advocating instruction in listening, the neglected language art, teachers at all levels have prepared material and used it effectively. *Their* students have profited. Unfortunately, most American students go through twelve years of schooling, and often four more years of instruction in college, without receiving direct instruction in the skills needed to listen accurately, purposefully, and critically. Some individual students somehow learn the needed skills: indirectly—through other assignments, casually—in related school activities, or desperately—in order to survive. Few attempts are made to organize an entire school for instruction in this predominant language art.

Listening instruction may be compared to the teaching of reading in the secondary school and composition instruction at all levels. Some teachers at all levels plan occasional lessons in writing; some high school teachers teach reading. But as survey after survey indicates, few schools currently boast of K–12 programs in either reading or writing. One feature does distinguish listening from reading and writing instruction: most American schools provide carefully sequenced programs in reading up through grade six, and most elementary school teachers do teach some of the elements of composition. Listening is still the neglected language art. It is, at best,

Scope and Sequence of Basic Listening Skills

Code: I Introduce
T Teach
R Review

Specific Skills	5	6	7	8	9	10	11	12
1. Determining one's purpose for listening	I	T	R	R	R	R	R	R
2. Guessing the speaker's purpose		I	T	T	T	T	R	R
3. Following a sequence of ideas and information	I	T	T	T	T	R	R	R
4. Noting details accurately	T	T	T	T	T	R	R	R
5. Following spoken directions	T	T	T	T	R	R	R	R
6. Guessing a speaker's plan of organization		I	I	T	T	T	T	T
7. Noting transitional expressions		I	I	T	T	R	R	R
8. Noting a speaker's main points	I	T	T	T	T	R	R	R
9. Noting a speaker's supporting examples	I	T	T	T	T	R	R	R
10. Keeping track of main points and examples by notetaking	I	I	T	T	T	R	R	R
11. Using a listening guide	I	I	T	T	T	T	R	R
12. Distinguishing between new and old ideas and material	I	I	T	T	T	T	R	R
13. Distinguishing between relevant and irrelevant material		I	T	T	T	R	R	R
14. Noting possible speaker bias			I	T	T	T	T	T
15. Noting emotional appeals			I	T	T	T	R	R
16. Distinguishing fact from opinion	I	I	T	T	T	T	R	R
17. Recognizing a speaker's inferences			I	I	T	T	T	T
18. Predicting outcomes of the talk	I	I	T	T	T	T	R	R
19. Drawing conclusions from the talk	I	I	T	T	T	T	R	R
20. Asking oneself questions while listening	T	T	T	T	R	R	R	R
21. Making personal associations	T	T	T	T	R	R	R	R
22. Summarizing a speaker's main points	I	I	T	T	T	T	T	T
23. Evaluating a speaker's competence to talk about a given subject		I	T	T	T	T	R	R
24. Noting use of propaganda devices		I	T	T	T	T	R	R
25. Predicting possible test questions	I	I	T	T	T	R	R	R

Figure 15. Scope and sequence of basic listening skills.

casually treated in elementary school and rarely an important instructional goal in the secondary school, despite the efforts of a few individual teachers who want their students to listen more effectively.

Six Suggestions for Starting a Program

Listening teachers who have successfully alerted their colleagues to the importance of listening instruction say that six steps are involved in setting up a total-school program:

1. Begin in one or two classes. As one teacher says, "Think big, but begin small." He points out the dangers in educating an entire teaching staff: "You dissipate your energies; you try to explain to too many people all at once, and they don't really know what you're getting at." His recommendation is to plan a "spectacularly, dramatically successful" program in one or two classes, get test evidence to show the program works, give demonstrations, encourage the students to spread the word, and, over a period of time, try to share enthusiasms with the staff.

2. Test to trigger interest. Students often fail to realize how poorly they listen until they see the results of their standardized tests. Teachers often fail to realize how ineffectively their own students listen until they see the results. Many listening teachers note that the best single way to generate interest in listening in a school is to administer a standardized test and share the results at a faculty meeting. However, the triggering test does not have to be commercially distributed. In one school, which today has an excellent program, the triggering device was a simple teacher-made test in critical listening that had been developed for an inservice course.

3. Set up a workshop. Many communities and school districts encourage, and sometimes mandate, inservice courses and workshops. Instead of a traditional topic, organize a program around some aspect of listening (accurate listening, lecture listening, or following spoken directions) and distribute reading lists and articles as well as copies of effective lessons. Invite a teacher or specialist from a nearby university or from a neighboring school, or simply share ideas from successful class experiences. (The References and Annotated List of Selected Teaching Materials found at the back of this book provide a variety of ideas and approaches.)

4. Involve students. Teachers who have initiated successful programs in their schools say that students are their best advertisements. One teacher says, "My best salesperson is a boy from the senior class who scored forty points below class average on our homemade listening test in September and who brought his score up to almost perfect by December." Student-made projects, charts, tests, and various graphics act as powerful inducements to skeptical colleagues. When a schoolwide scope and sequence is discussed by the faculty, students should be present to comment, edit, and advise. Always, when teaching material is assembled, highlight student input.

5. Involve parents and the community. Many business people are concerned today about the listening skills of employees. Many companies purchase materials designed to improve listening skills on the job. If possible, some of the materials used in business and industry should be examined in faculty discussions of listening. It sometimes helps to convince an uninterested colleague by noting that Xerox and IBM have invested in costly programs to teach the very skills listed on the school's scope and sequence chart. When parents with an interest in listening can be identified, they also should be involved in program planning.

6. Set up a clearinghouse. As individual teachers create more and better material in listening instruction, they should be encouraged to file copies in a central clearinghouse. Each teacher's ideas and exercises may be studied and serve as catalysts for other ideas. The school's scope and sequence chart acts as a general guide to grade-level placement of skills; lesson ideas are always a teacher's own, but the activities of colleagues may provide stimulation and model lessons. The file can be augmented by articles reproduced from professional journals; a teacher finding a new article on teaching listening can place a copy in the file.

Using these six steps as guidelines, teachers can produce an effective schoolwide program in the mastery of basic listening skills. Students can be successfully taught to be sensitive, skilled listeners both in school and in their daily lives.

REFERENCES

Anderson, John R. *Cognitive Psychology and Its Implications.* San Francisco: W. H. Freeman, 1980.

This college textbook, selected as one of the outstanding books of the year by the editors of *Psychology Today,* presents much of the theoretical background for recent research in listening and language study.

Anderson, Paul S., and Dianne Lapp. *Language Skills in Elementary Education.* New York: Macmillan, 1979.

This general perspective of language arts in the schools contains excellent ideas for teaching basic listening skills.

Ausubel, David P. "The Use of Advance Organizers in the Learning and Retention of Meaningful Verbal Material." *Journal of Educational Psychology* 51 (1960): 267-72.

Ausubel, a Yale psychologist, researched the effect of advance organizers. His article explains the theory behind their use.

Castallo, Richard. "Listening Guide: A First Step toward Notetaking and Listening Skills." *Journal of Reading* 19 (1976): 289-90 (ERIC No. EJ 129 220).

The author discusses the value of listening guides and shows how they may be developed.

Devine, Thomas G. "Listening." *Review of Educational Research* 37 (1967): 153-58.

A careful examination of research in listening instruction, factors affecting reading and listening, and tests in the area.

Devine, Thomas G. "Reading and Listening: New Research Findings." *Elementary English* 45 (1968): 346-48.

This article reexamines the belief that instruction in listening affects competence in reading and that reading instruction affects listening.

Devine, Thomas G. "Listening: What Do We Know after Fifty Years of Research and Theorizing?" *Journal of Reading* 21 (1978): 296-304 (ERIC No. EJ 169 540).

One of the most complete surveys of the research in listening, the article tries to pinpoint what is really known in contrast to what is guessed at.

Devine, Thomas G. "Listening in the Classroom." In *Teaching Study Skills: A Guide for Teachers.* Boston: Allyn and Bacon, 1981.

A variety of practical teaching ideas are presented within the framework of a book on study skills.

Duker, Sam. *Listening: Readings.* Metuchen, N.J.: Scarecrow Press, 1966. *Listening: Readings II.* Metuchen, N.J.: Scarecrow Press, 1971 (ERIC Document Reproduction Service No. ED 053 151).

These two volumes present dozens of important articles written about the teaching of listening. Having them in a school collection saves much library searching.

Duker, Sam. *Listening Bibliography.* 2d ed. Metuchen, N.J.: Scarecrow Press, 1968 (ERIC Document Reproduction Service No. ED 053 150).

This annotated bibliography contains 1,332 references. It is invaluable to researchers and teachers in the field.

Green, Harry A., and Walter P. Petty. *Developing Language Skills in the Elementary Schools.* 4th ed. Boston: Allyn and Bacon, 1971.

The authors include dozens of good ideas for teaching listening skills within the context of the total school language arts program.

Landry, Donald L. "The Neglect of Listening." *Elementary English* 46 (1969): 599-605 (ERIC No. EJ 005 206).

The article examines the reasons for the neglect of listening in schools. It provides valuable information for those arguing the need for listening programs.

Lundsteen, Sara W. *Children Learn to Communicate.* Englewood Cliffs, N.J.: Prentice-Hall, 1976 (ERIC Document Reproduction Service No. ED 116 220).

The central focus of the book is an approach to language arts through creative problem solving for which listening is a subskill.

Lundsteen, Sara W. *Listening: Its Impact on Reading and the Other Language Arts.* Urbana, Ill.: National Council of Teachers of English, 1979 (ERIC Document Reproduction Service No. ED 169 537).

Lundsteen, an outstanding authority in listening, looks at theory and practice. This is a "must" book for listening teachers.

Moffett, James. *A Student-Centered Language Arts Curriculum, Grades K-13: A Handbook for Teachers.* Boston: Houghton Mifflin, 1968.

The author includes many excellent ideas for developing speaking-listening skills at all grade levels.

Morrow, James, and Murray Suid. *Real-World Learning*

in the Schools. Rochelle Park, N.J.: Hayden Book Co., 1977.

This is a rich collection of teaching ideas growing out of media approaches to learning. Many of the ideas lead to superb listening activities.

Palmatier, Robert A. "A Notetaking System for Learning." *Journal of Reading* 17 (1973): 36-39 (ERIC No. EJ 084 375).

The author presents ideas for teaching notetaking, all based on research in study skills.

Pauk, Walter. *How to Study in College.* 2d ed. Boston: Houghton Mifflin, 1974.

Pauk, director of the study skills program at Cornell University, shares hundreds of ideas for improving study skills; some of the best pertain to listening in the lecture class.

Russell, David H., and E. F. Russell. *Listening Aids through the Grades.* New York: Bureau of Publications, Teachers College, Columbia University, 1959.

Here are more than 100 useful ideas in listening, divided by grade level and type of skill. Every listening teacher should have access to this book.

Savage, John F. *Effective Communications: Language Arts Instruction in the Elementary School.* Chicago: Science Research Associates, 1977 (ERIC Document Reproduction Service No. ED 145 424).

This excellent book on teaching language arts con-tains creative and exciting activities in listening. A valuable addition to the listening teacher's library.

Shafer, Robert E. "Will Psycholinguistics Change Reading in Secondary Schools?" *Journal of Reading* 21 (1978): 305-16 (ERIC No. EJ 169 541).

This article gives a brief, understandable summary of the controversy about the skills approach. It should be read by all planning a scope and sequence in listening—or reading.

Smith, James A. *Adventures in Communication: Language Arts Methods.* Boston: Allyn and Bacon, 1972.

Smith includes hundreds of specific strategies for teaching listening skills as well as a good theoretical view of the whole language arts program.

Thomas, Keith J., and Charles K. Cummings. "The Efficacy of Listening Guides: Some Preliminary Findings with Tenth and Eleventh Graders." *Journal of Reading* 21 (1978): 705-709 (ERIC No. EJ 181 352).

The authors describe research in the use of listening guides and also pointers on how to develop and use them.

Weber, Kenneth J. *Yes, They Can! A Practical Guide for Teaching the Adolescent Slower Learner.* Toronto, Canada: Methuen, 1974.

A treasure trove of good teaching ideas for all kinds of learners. The material on listening and thinking is especially valuable.

AN ANNOTATED LIST OF SELECTED TEACHING MATERIALS

Many publishers now distribute excellent instructional materials in listening. Representative items are listed and briefly described below.

Countdown for Listening. Lakeland, Fla.: Educational Development Corporation, 1961.
> These six cassette tapes include twenty-four separate lessons and a teacher's guide. Useful in middle grades.

Critical Reading and Listening (CRL) Program. Huntington Station, N.Y.: Instructional/Communications Technology, Inc.
> More than 600 graded skill lessons (in kits and on cassette tapes) relate reading and listening skills development in literal understanding, interpretation, analysis, evaluation, appreciation, and application.

HM Study Skills Program. Reston, Va.: National Association of Secondary School Principals.
> Two programs (I for grades 5, 6, and 7; II for 8, 9, and 10) focus on nine study skills areas; each includes a separate section on listening. Student texts are supplemented by a teacher's guide and material for conducting inservice workshops.

Listening. Los Angeles: Churchill Film.
> This is a fourteen-minute film aimed at intermediate grades. Use for consciousness raising.

Listening-Reading Program. Lexington, Mass.: D. C. Heath and Co.
> An entire "minisystem" series with kits for grades 1–6; each includes records, response sheets, and other aids.

Listening Skills Program. Chicago: Science Research Associates.
> A set of thirty-six long-playing records covering a range of skills and offering a variety of materials.

Listening Skills Program. Chicago: Science Research Associates.
> A related set of filmstrips and twelve cassette tapes at three levels. Both SRA series are useful for middle school students.

Listening Skills Program. Englewood Cliffs, N.J.: Scholastic Book Services.
> Unit I (for grades 1–3) aims at sixteen listening skills; Unit II (for grades 4–6) at fourteen. Each unit contains forty taped short stories on ten cassettes, a set of forty illustrated worksheets on spirit masters, and a teacher's guide.

Sourcetapes. Princeton, N.J.: Sourcetapes.
> Interesting tape recordings, sometimes of actual events with real voices. Useful as material for teacher-made exercises and lessons.

Spoken Arts Multi-Media. Orange City, Fla.: Rancourt and Company.
> Cassette Library I contains fifty tapes of fairy tales, poetry, and stories for young children; Cassette Library II contains fifty tapes aimed at middle school and junior high classes. Tapes may be purchased separately. Useful as material for teacher-made lessons.

Tune-In Listening/Reading Program. Pleasantville, N.Y.: Sunburst Communications.
> Four boxes each contain four thirty-minute radio shows (for example, "The Lone Ranger" and "The Shadow") plus scripts for the programs and a teacher's guide. Reading level is grade 4, but interest level extends into middle school and junior high.

Old-Time Radio Cassettes. Pleasantville, N.Y.: Sunburst Communications.
> Each one-hour recording contains two or more complete radio programs, many with original commercials. Examples include: "The Aldrich Family," "Mr. Keen," "Fibber McGee and Molly," and "The Green Hornet." Useful for teacher-made lessons and activities.

Your Communication Skills. Chicago: Coronet Films.
> This eleven-minute film provides a good introduction to listening for middle school students.

AUTHOR

Thomas G. Devine is Professor of Education at the University of Lowell. Formerly he coordinated the English and Language Arts Program at Boston University. His latest book is *Teaching Study Skills: A Guide to Teachers;* other publications include secondary school and college textbooks and numerous articles in professional journals. Dr. Devine has been a member of the Board of Directors of the National Council of Teachers of English and has served on NCTE's Committee on Research. He is the recipient of the 1982 F. Andre Favat Award of the Massachusetts Council of Teachers of English.